PORTSMOUTH'S
WORLD WAR TWO HEROES

PORTSMOUTH'S
WORLD WAR TWO HEROES
Stories of the Fallen Men and Women

JAMES DALY

The
History
Press

This book is dedicated to:

Private Henry Miller (1922–95)
Royal Berkshire Regiment, Parachute Regiment and Royal Army Ordnance Corps
1942–47 (Iraq, Palestine, Arnhem, prisoner of war in Germany)

Leading Stoker Thomas Daly (1920–43)
Royal Navy 1940–43 (HMS *Enterprise*, SS *Laconia*, interned in Vichy North Africa)

And the thousands of other men and women from Portsmouth
involved in and affected by the Second World War.

Cover illustrations: front: top: A British Royal Navy 'T'-class destroyer
steams next to the US aircraft carrier USS *Wasp* (CV-18) in August
1945. (US Navy National Museum of Naval Aviation photo No
1977.031.074.099); *bottom:* Royal Engineers prepare to embark on to
a landing craft on a temporary pier alongside South Parade Pier. (*The
News*, Portsmouth, 2945). *Back:* Portsmouth's World War Two Memorial,
unveiled in 2005. (Author's collection)

First published 2012

The History Press
The Mill, Brimscombe Port
Stroud, Gloucestershire, GL5 2QG
www.thehistorypress.co.uk

© James Daly, 2012

The right of James Daly to be identified as the Author
of this work has been asserted in accordance with the
Copyrights, Designs and Patents Act 1988.

British Library Cataloguing in Publication Data.
A catalogue record for this book is available from the British Library.

ISBN 978 0 7524 6351 3

Typesetting and origination by The History Press
Printed in Great Britain
Manufacturing managed by Jellyfish Print Solutions Ltd

Contents

List of Illustrations   6

Acknowledgements   8

Abbreviations   10

Introduction   11

PART ONE – THE ROYAL NAVY

1   'Duty nobly done': Chief Petty Officer Reginald Ellingworth GC   15

2   The Battleships: HMS *Royal Oak*, HMS *Hood* and HMS *Barham*   23

3   Portsmouth's Boy Sailors   33

4   'Most promising, should go far': Lieutenant Commander William
      Hussey DSO, DSC   36

5   Portsmouth's Submariners   42

6   *Per Mar Per Terram*: The Royal Marines   48

PART TWO – THE ARMY

7   Pompey's Tigers: The Hampshire Regiment   54

8   'Very great powers of command': Major Robert Easton DSO, MBE   61

9   Overlord: D-Day and the Battle of Normandy   67

10 Prisoners of War   76

11 Forgotten Army: War in the Far East   82

PART THREE – THE ROYAL AIR FORCE

12 'Bucky': Wing Commander John Buchanan DSO, DFC   87

13 Portsmouth's Bomber Boys   92

14 'Nine Gun': Flight Lieutenant John Coghlan DFC   100

15 Brothers in Arms: The Venables Brothers   106

PART FOUR – THE OTHER SERVICES

16 The NAAFI   108

17 Women at War   113

18 The Merchant Navy   119

Notes   126

Bibliography   137

Index   141

List of Illustrations

Portsmouth's Second World War Memorial. *(Author)*

Chief Petty Officer Reg Ellingworth GC. *(Trevor Ellingworth)*

Reg Ellingworth's grave in Milton Cemetery, Portsmouth. *(Author)*

Frederick Bealing, pictured as a young seaman. *(Doris Bealing)*

Frederick Bealing in tropical uniform as an older sailor. *(Doris Bealing)*

Families read a list of men killed on HMS *Royal Oak*. *(The News 174)*

The main gate to Portsmouth Dockyard. *(Author)*

HMS *Hood*. *(Michael Mason/HMS Hood Association)*

HMS *Barham* explodes. *(Imperial War Museum FLM/1984)*

Portsmouth Naval Memorial on Southsea Common. *(Author)*

HMS *Lively* in Malta. *(Imperial War Museum GM/165)*

Able Seaman Henry Miller GC. *(RN Submarine Museum)*

Electrical Artificer Arthur Bigglestone DSM and Bar. *(RN Submarine Museum)*

A Royal Marine kissing his partner goodbye. *(The News 197)*

Colour Sergeant Frederick Bird's grave in Highland Road Cemetery, Portsmouth. *(Author)*

The grave of Private George Gillard in St Mary's churchyard, Portchester. *(Author)*

Men of the 1st Battalion, the Hampshire Regiment, relaxing in Palestine early in the war. *(Kath Connick)*

Hampshires relaxing with a drink in the Middle East. *(Kath Connick)*

Major Robert Easton DSO, MBE. *(Portsmouth Grammar School)*

The grave of Lance Corporal Leslie Webb MM in Milton Cemetery, Portsmouth. *(Author)*

Private Bobby Johns. *(Portsmouth Museums and Records Service)*

Sergeant Sidney Cornell DCM. *(Portsmouth Museums and Records Service 2010/598)*

A statue of a British soldier in Normandy. *(Author)*

The D-Day Memorial Stone in Southsea, Portsmouth. *(Author)*

A postcard sent by Private William Starling. *(Portsmouth Museums and Records Service)*

Wing Commander John Buchanan DSO, DFC. *(Portsmouth Grammar School)*

Flight Lieutenant Patrick McCarthy. *(Chrissie Lynn)*

A letter sent by the adjutant of 7 Squadron to Patrick McCarthy's mother. *(Chrissie Lynn)*

The Runnymede Memorial. *(Steve Poole, Flickr user Stavioni)*

Flight Lieutenant John Coghlan DFC. *(www.acesofww2.com)*

The grave of Canteen Manager George Huggins in Kingston Cemetery, Portsmouth. *(Author)*

Kingston Cemetery, Portsmouth. *(Author)*

Wrens on parade at HMS *Vernon*. *(Portsmouth Museums and Records Service)*

The grave of Private Audrey Leppard in Kingston Cemetery, Portsmouth. *(Author)*

ATS girls manning a 3.7in anti-aircraft gun site near Portsmouth. *(The News)*

The grave of Engineer Officer Albert Lofting in Kingston Cemetery, Portsmouth. *(Author)*

The SS *Portsdown*. *(Ian Boyle of Simplon Postcards)*

The Swashway Channel. *(Author)*

The grave of Seth Burgess in Milton Cemetery, Portsmouth. *(Author)*

The Tower Hill Memorial, London. *(Iain McLauchlan)*

Acknowledgements

DURING THE TIME taken to research and write this book I have been fortunate enough to receive the help of many people, for which I am very grateful.

I would like to thank the relatives who I have been fortunate enough to correspond with during my research. The following kindly shared their families' experiences with me: Doris Bealing, the daughter of Petty Officer Frederick Bealing of HMS *Royal Oak*; Chrissie Lynn, the niece of Flight Lieutenant Patrick McCarthy DFC; Chris Eldgridge, the nephew of Ordinary Seaman Ray Green of HMS *Barham*; Trevor Ellingworth, grandson of Chief Petty Officer Reg Ellingworth GC; Chris Cornell, a descendant of Sergeant Sid Cornell DCM; Kath Connick, a descendant of Corporal Mark Pook MM, and Stephen Harding-Morris, whose family were friends of Flying Officer Guy Venables. I would also like to thank the individuals who have taken part in oral history interviews with Portsmouth City Museums over the years – their reminiscences add so much to our understanding of the experiences of past generations.

John Sadden, the archivist at Portsmouth Grammar School, kindly shared information on Old Portmuthians who were killed during the war. Much of the information has been compiled by pupils at the school, who are to be congratulated for their work. I would also like to thank The National Archives, the RAF Museum, Dagenham Libraries and the Tank Museum, Bovington.

Stephen Fogden kindly shared copies of National Archives documents relating to Private George Sullivan and the Chindits, and Nana Chiba very kindly translated the documents from Japanese. The late Ian Daglish also shared useful information relating to the Battle of Normandy. Members of the forum on www.ww2talk.com were extremely helpful during my initial research.

Joe Fukuto of the website World War Two Aces, Debbie Corner at the Royal Naval Submarine Museum, Frank Allen of the HMS *Hood* Association, Ian Boyle of Simplon Postcards, Dean Kedward of the *The News*, and Flickr users Steve Poole and Iain McLauchlan very kindly assisted with images. I would like to thank my colleagues at Portsmouth City

Museums and Records Service for their thoughts, suggestions and assistance with images, in particular Archivist John Stedman, Military History Officer Andrew Whitmarsh and Collections Manager Rosalinda Hardiman. The staff at Portsmouth Central Library were helpful as ever, in particular Alan King and Gill Ferrett in the library's History Centre. The library's naval collection is a real treasure, and one of the best resources for naval history easily accessible to the general public.

Peter Daly, Scott Daly, John Erickson and Andrew Whitmarsh kindly proofread chapters and made valuable comments on the text. Any mistakes that remain are entirely my own.

Last, and certainly by no means least, I would like to thank my family and my girlfriend Sarah for their invaluable support.

June 2011
Portsmouth

Abbreviations

ADM	Admiralty
AIR	Air Ministry
AL	*Army List*
AFL	*Air Force List*
BDL	Barking and Dagenham Library
BDR	*Barking and Dagenham Recorder*
BT	Board of Trade
EN	*Portsmouth Evening News*
GRO	General Register Office
HO	Home Office
LG	*London Gazette*
NL	*Navy List*
OHI	Oral History Interview
PCL	Portsmouth Central Library
PGS	Portsmouth Grammar School
PMRS	Portsmouth Museums and Records Service
PREM	Prime Minister
RMAS	Royal Military Academy Sandhurst
TNA	The National Archives
WO	War Office

Introduction

We in Portsmouth know quite well what war means. Indeed, there are few cities and towns to which war has a deeper meaning.
    – Alderman Sir Denis Daley, Lord Mayor of Portsmouth during the Second World War

AS MANY AS 2,549 men and women from Portsmouth are known to have been killed while serving with the armed forces during the Second World War. Given the manner in which war dead are recorded, the true figure is likely to be even higher. These numbers are not just statistics; they are not even just names. They are real people, whose loss had a huge impact on partners, children, parents, relations, friends and comrades, and, until recently, their sacrifice has gone virtually unnoticed in their home city.

My interest in the Second World War stems from the experiences of my granddad and my great-uncle in two very different theatres. My granddad served in the Parachute Regiment, and was wounded and captured at Arnhem. My great-uncle, Tommy, was on board the troopship SS *Laconia* when she was torpedoed in the South Atlantic, and he died months later from an illness that he picked up while a prisoner of war in North Africa.

My granddad died when I was 11 years old, and obviously I never got to meet my great-uncle, so finding out about what happened to them was a natural step towards finding out about my family and where I came from. However, it also got me thinking: these were the experiences of just two men from Portsmouth, so what about the thousands of others? What happened to them had a lasting effect on both sides of my family – only when we multiply that effect by thousands do we begin to understand just how much war can change society forever.

Many of Britain's war memorials date from the period after the end of the First World War. After this conflict, the like of which had never been seen before, the British public felt a collective need to grieve publicly for their losses. Memorials up and down the country contain row upon row of the names of the fallen, and Portsmouth is no exception. The city's Cenotaph and War Memorial were unveiled in 1921, and had been funded by donations made by the public – ordinary men and women who wished to remember the city folk who had made the ultimate sacrifice.

Yet by the end of the Second World War in 1945, Britain was virtually exhausted. After another long and bloody struggle there seems to have been little desire or enthusiasm for more memorials. Portsmouth had been devastated by bombing, and understandably local people wanted to rebuild and get on with their lives. In Portsmouth the Second World War was marked only by the addition of a simple plaque to the First World War Memorial. For sixty years, the names of the men and women from Portsmouth who were killed went unrecorded. Thankfully the centrepiece for Portsmouth's Second World War Memorial was unveiled in 2005, and a fundraising campaign is under way to enable the names of the fallen to be recorded in perpetuity. Part of the appeal for a memorial in Portsmouth involved the city council compiling a list of names of Portsmouth men and women who died between 1939 and 1947 – the years recognised by the Commonwealth War Graves Commission. Having checked that my great-uncle Tommy was on the list, it occurred to me that each of the thousands of names was, in fact, somebody else's 'Great-Uncle Tommy'. All of them had their own story, and together their experiences would tell the story of a lost generation.

From the basic details on the city council's list I searched for their entries on the commission's online Debt of Honour Register. This gave a lot of information about each name: their rank, age, unit, date of death, cemetery, and any awards and other information. With the use of a remarkable website called Geoff's Search Engine, I was able to search the commission's records and found even more Portsmouth men who had until now slipped through the net. Local war memorials, such as those in parish churches, also produced more names.

From there, some more detailed research shed light on the bare details. Researching Second World War servicemen is by no means a simple task. Service records are only in the public domain for some older sailors and Royal Marines; the majority of Second World War service records remain available only to next of kin. Sadly, it is much easier to research servicemen if they were officers, and even more so if they won medals or fought in famous battles. And it is even more tragic that it is much easier to research servicemen who died during the war compared to those who survived.

Despite the difficulties in finding information, some incredible stories emerged. Between them they tell the story of the Second World War, and the lives of the people of Portsmouth in wartime. Regrettably, due to constraints of space, it is impossible to tell all of their stories in detail, but I hope that the men and women I have written about here stand as representatives for their generation; a generation who stood up to be counted when it mattered. That any name is not mentioned is by no means a suggestion that their sacrifice was not important; indeed, there are many fascinating stories that are yet to be told. Due to the complex nature of the war, in some cases there are crossovers between chapters – for example, men who fought and were captured in the Far East or men of the Hampshire Regiment who fought in Normandy. I hope their stories have been told in the most suitable context.

A few statistics regarding Portsmouth's Second World War dead should help to place things in context: the youngest was only 16, and the oldest was 73. They died in forty-seven countries, in Europe, Africa, the Near East, the Far East and North America, and in virtually every ocean and sea on the globe. Almost every corner of the world has a small field or patch of water that will forever be part of the history of Portsmouth.

Less people were killed in the Second World War than in the First World War; nevertheless, the losses suffered between 1939 and 1947 had a profound impact upon both Portsmouth as a city and the individual people and families who lived there. Every area of Portsmouth suffered losses, and very few people would have not known at least one person who was killed.

Portsmouth's Second World War Memorial, unveiled in 2005. *(Author)*

Portsmouth had a population of over 200,000 in 1939, and although losses of 2,549 men and women might not sound excessive by comparison, we need to remember that this figure consists of a significant amount of the city's young adult men.

A total of 154 men from Portsmouth who fell in the Second World War won some kind of decoration, but the majority of men died unrewarded. For every heroic story, there are plenty more ordinary men and women who died doing what they had to do. They might not have thought of themselves as heroes; indeed, I have never heard or read of any veterans describing themselves as heroes. But to us, their grateful descendants, they are heroes. Ordinary people who did extraordinary things deserve our respect and remembrance.

Not surprisingly, more men from Portsmouth were killed serving with the Royal Navy than any other service. In total 1,290 naval officers, ratings and Wrens from the city died during the Second World War, performing every kind of role imaginable in the senior service. It is noticeable that many of the naval ratings from Portsmouth were older, experienced men who had been born elsewhere but moved to the city while in the navy. Portsmouth also provided many Royal Marines, with 116 being lost.

A total of 675 men from Portsmouth died serving with the British army, as infantry, tank crew, engineers, gunners, cooks, commandos, paras, glider pilots, guardsmen, pioneers, chaplains, medics and signallers. Not many of these men were regular soldiers, as the pre-war British army was small and only expanded once war was declared. The Royal Air Force also expanded considerably in wartime and 410 airmen from Portsmouth were killed, including many bomber aircrew. We should not forget either the sacrifice of other lesser-known services, in particular the Merchant Navy, the NAAFI, WRNS and ATS.

What is meant by 'from Portsmouth'? Given that Portsmouth is a port city from which people have come and gone for hundreds of years, the term can be applied quite loosely. Many people were born elsewhere but found themselves stationed in Portsmouth, and then put down roots. Many are born here and then move away, but retain their Pompey heritage. Others might have married a local girl, been educated here or had relations here. All deserve to be remembered as sons and daughters of Portsmouth.

PART ONE
THE ROYAL NAVY

1

'Duty nobly done': Chief Petty Officer Reginald Ellingworth GC

MOST PEOPLE WOULD assume that to earn one of the country's highest decorations for bravery, the winner must have fought in the maelstrom of battle and killed scores of the enemy. Yet remarkably, not only did Reg Ellingworth never fire a shot in anger, but he never even left Britain. Yet the courage and devotion to duty that he showed was perhaps the most impressive of all.

Reginald Vincent Ellingworth was born in Wolverhampton on 28 January 1898,[1] the son of Frank and Kate Ellingworth. Early twentieth-century Wolverhampton was home to a number of car manufacturers, and after leaving school Reg Ellingworth worked as a motorcar body maker. His career in the motor industry was short-lived, however, because at the age of 16 Ellingworth joined the Royal Navy as a boy seaman. He enlisted in 1913, shortly before the outbreak of the First World War. His service record states that he was just over 5ft 3in tall, with brown hair and grey eyes. He was initially rated as a boy second class.

Ellingworth's initial service was spent on the training hulks HMS *Impregnable* and HMS *Powerful*, both moored in Plymouth. After several years of training, he was promoted to boy seaman first class, and in 1914 was posted to HMS *Benbow*, an Iron Duke-class battleship, on which he was present at the Battle of Jutland in 1916. Whilst on the *Benbow* Ellingworth reached the age of 18 in January 1916, and joined the Royal Navy fully for an engagement of twelve years. Shortly afterwards, in March 1916, he was promoted to able seaman.

In July 1917, when Ellingworth was still only 19, he transferred from HMS *Benbow* to HMS *Dolphin*, the Royal Navy submarine establishment at Gosport, and in December 1917 joined the crew of submarine *L2*. The submarine was still in its infancy as a mode of warfare and early submarines were small and dangerous, while their crews were part of a close-knit community. The early submarines were given numbers rather than names, and the depot ships to which they were attached carried the HMS prefix. Accordingly, in December 1917, *L2* was attached to HMS *Ambrosia*, and then in September 1919 to HMS *Titania*. Also in 1919, Ellingworth married his first wife, Rose, in Barrow-in-Furness.[2] The Vickers shipbuilding

Chief Petty Officer Reg Ellingworth GC. *(Trevor Ellingworth)*

yard in Barrow was a centre for submarine construction, and perhaps this is why Ellingworth was there.

Ellingworth's early years in the Royal Navy were mainly spent on board submarines and submarine depot ships, apart from several years on board HMS *Benbow* and the deployment to Ceylon (Sri Lanka) on board HMS *Serafin*. He also spent several spells at shore establishments such as HMS *Dolphin*, HMS *Vernon* and HMS *Victory*.

He was obviously happy serving in the Royal Navy, for in 1927 he had re-engaged for a further period of service. By then, at the age of 29, he had grown to 5ft 10in, and had tattoos on both arms – a hallmark of a career sailor. After his first wife died at the young age of 24,[3] Ellingworth married his second wife Jessie in Portsmouth in 1925.[4]

Unfortunately, Ellingworth's service record is only available up until 1928. By that time he was a petty officer, and had settled in Portsmouth with a family. He was well on the way to becoming the kind of experienced, long-serving sailor that formed the backbone of the Royal Navy in wartime. A high proportion of the sailors from Portsmouth who served in the Second World War were older men, many of whom had also served in the First World War. Many – such as Ellingworth – did not originally come from Portsmouth, but had settled there after joining the Royal Navy. This shows just how transient Portsmouth society was, with people coming from all over Britain – and beyond – to serve in the Royal Navy. From 1934 onwards Reg Ellingworth and his family were living at 187 Powerscourt Road in Copnor, and some time in 1939 or 1940 his family moved to 362 Copnor Road.[5]

It is not surprising that, having spent much of his career on board submarines, and having already been based at HMS *Vernon* on several occasions, Ellingworth was seconded to work in mine warfare. HMS *Vernon* was the Royal Navy's Torpedo and Mine Warfare School, and it had also assumed responsibility for defusing enemy mines.

Bomb disposal in Britain during the Second World War began in a fragmentary state, with no agreement between the armed services as to who would deal with what. After much discussion, it was decided that the Royal Air Force would take responsibility for bombs that landed on airfields, the Royal Navy for bombs that landed in dockyards and in water up to the high-tide mark, while the Royal Engineers would dispose of bombs that landed anywhere else. The one notable exception, however, was when the Luftwaffe began dropping magnetic sea mines on land by parachute during the summer and autumn of 1940, and the Royal Navy's Rendering Mines Safe (RMS) experts were called upon due to their experience of handling mines. Guidelines laid down by the War Office and the Admiralty stated that whilst parties of naval personnel were responsible for disarming mines, Royal Engineers bomb disposal squads were to carry out any digging required and then dispose of the mines once they had been made safe.[6]

Unexploded bombs and mines came in two forms: bombs that failed to detonate successfully and those that were deliberately set to explode after a delay. Both could be extremely hazardous and disruptive to civilians and the emergency services, and not least to the men who were detailed to dispose of them. One historian has referred to parachute mines as 'the most fearsome weapon of the Blitz'.[7] The manner in which they slowly floated to earth meant that they were impossible to drop with any accuracy; hence the destruction that they caused was completely random. The need to cordon off and evacuate areas around unexploded mines caused severe disruption, and the demands on navy, army and air force bomb disposal crews were extremely heavy during the German air attacks on British towns and cities in 1940. The RMS department from HMS *Vernon* consisted of twelve teams, each of one officer and a senior rating as his assistant[8]. Reg Ellingworth served as assistant to Lieutenant Commander Richard Ryan. Although Ryan was the senior officer, the two men always faced the same dangers – any mine that might have exploded would make no distinction between the officer and his assistant.

Ryan and Ellingworth did not have long to wait to tackle their first mines. On 30 April 1940 a German 'accidental' air raid on Clacton, Essex, caused the first civilian deaths in Britain from enemy action. The intention of a lone Heinkel bomber had been to attack shipping by dropping mines in the Thames Estuary, but due to thick fog the two mines were dropped on Clacton, and after being engaged by anti-aircraft guns the Heinkel crashed. One of the mines exploded, killing and injuring many. During the next day the emergency services worked to clear the damage, and found what they believed to be a hot-water cylinder in one house. One of the rescue workers noticed German writing on the 'cylinder'.[9] The Royal Navy were called, and Lieutenant Commander Ryan and Chief Petty Officer Ellingworth identified it as a new 'C'-type parachute mine, which was safely defused and taken away for further examination. The mine recovered at Clacton was, in fact, the first example of a 'C'-type mine to be captured and defused intact, and by rendering it safe Ryan and Ellingworth had given experts the opportunity to examine it and work out how to counter it. Their actions at Clacton saved many lives by uncovering the mine's secrets.

The two men went on to defuse hundreds of bombs and mines together throughout 1940, earning a reputation for bravery and coolness in the face of danger. Defusing mines was clearly an incredibly dangerous duty – on 6 August 1940 a booby-trapped mine exploded whilst being examined in a shed at HMS *Vernon*, killing one officer and four ratings.

The fuse presented the biggest hazard in attempting to render a mine safe. Within the fuse itself an arming clock controlled the timing of the explosion, usually around twenty-two seconds after landing. Even more dangerous, however, was the possibility of the mine failing to go off at all, which meant that the fuse might have been delayed and might then re-activate at any time. Any sudden movement – such as those typically required to dispose of an unexploded mine – might cause a detonation. In this event, both Ryan and Ellingworth would have known that they would probably have had a maximum of twenty-two seconds, which was nowhere near enough time to escape out of the blast zone. As the mines were magnetic, no metal – including tools – could be brought near them whilst still live. Information passed to Air Raid Precaution personnel by the Ministry of Home Security suggests that parachute mines took on average forty-five minutes to defuse, depending on whether access was difficult or whether any digging was involved.[10] Gradually, the Germans also fitted anti-handling fuses to their mines in order to prevent them being captured intact. The message was clear and chilling – the Germans were trying to kill the bomb disposal men themselves.

Most of the early mines dealt with by the Royal Navy had been dropped on land in error, but on 17 September 1940 the Germans suddenly began to drop large numbers of 'C'-type mines on land deliberately as part of the Blitz. Between 17 September and 22 October 1940, 318 parachute mines were dropped on Britain, mainly on London and the East Coast. The Home Office estimated that about half of them did not explode.[11] This new wave of mines was deemed so serious that Winston Churchill ordered the Chiefs of Staff to consider retaliatory mine attacks on German towns and cities.[12] Later in October 1940, Churchill admitted in a memo that 'it is true that we have been much vexed by the issue of parachute mines'.[13]

There were initial concerns that the Germans were attempting to mine the River Thames, but that their aircraft were baulking in the face of anti-aircraft defences and jettisoning their mines on land. This, however, proved not to be the case – their dropping on land was a deliberate new tactic.[14] Immediately after the new wave of parachute mines in September 1940, the War Cabinet ordered that press reports regarding them should be blocked. This was partly to prevent the Germans from realising just how destructive they were, but also to keep secret the fact that many of them had not exploded, and that the RMS teams were working on defusing them.[15] Royal Navy teams from HMS *Vernon* were routinely called in to deal with defusing sea mines that had been dropped on land, and from mid-September Ryan and Ellingworth were based in London, staying at the Royal Automobile Club in Pall Mall.[16]

Ellingworth worked mainly with Lieutenant Commander Ryan, although in one incident he worked with Lieutenant C.A. Hodges to make safe a magnetic mine that had fallen on oyster beds in Whitstable, Kent. Ryan and Ellingworth made an excellent team and they worked on unexploded mines throughout the summer of 1940, as far away as Liverpool, Sheffield and Cardiff, but mainly in London and its surrounding area.[17] In another notable incident, Ryan and Ellingworth worked on and defused six magnetic mines. One of them had fallen into a canal and Ryan waded in up to his waist, fumbling in the thick mud before managing to locate the mine and neutralise the fuse.[18]

In an incident at Hornchurch, Essex, Ryan and Ellingworth safely defused a mine that had landed near an RAF airfield and a munitions factory. They had been called urgently by the station commander, Wing Commander Cecil Bouchier and his recollections tell us much about their work:

It was a fearsomely long oblong cylindrical object, nearly half as long as a petrol tanker lorry on the road. I watched him [Ryan] rope off a large area … thereafter I watched his slow approach along to the forbidding object where he put his stethoscope to it. Then after a long while, with great patience and careful, sensitive fingers, he withdrew from the 'block busting' monster its timing device and detonator which he later handed to me as a souvenir … Had it gone off it would have blown much of my Hornchurch station to bits. When I thanked him he said that he could not stop for a drink or a meal. He had to hurry to Dagenham nearby …[19]

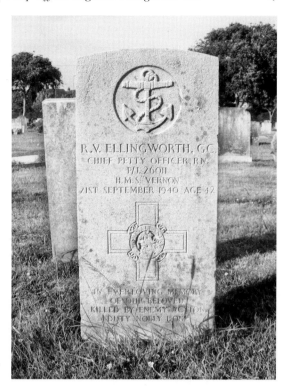

Reg Ellingworth's grave in Milton
Cemetery, engraved with the George Cross.
(*Author*)

Ryan and Ellingworth went straight from Hornchurch to Dagenham, where on 21 September 1940 the Luftwaffe had launched a heavy bombing raid. Along with the usual high-explosive and incendiary bombs, a number of parachute mines were also dropped.[20] Two RMS teams were sent to Dagenham: Ryan and Ellingworth, and Commander R.V. Moore and his assistant.[21] Ryan and Ellingworth went to tackle a parachute mine suspended from the roof of a house in Oval Road.[22] Mr J. Millar was a schoolboy at the time:

> We came out of the Anderson shelter and we were told by the Police and ARP wardens that the whole district had to be evacuated … For some reason or other we were rather late in evacuating our house and everybody else had gone and the streets were cordoned off while the bomb disposal team went to work … I decided that I wanted to have a look at the landmine so I nipped out of the house and bypassed the Police barricades by going through the back entries … I was able to look at the bomb disposal team starting to work on the mine … I was very impressed with their calmness …[23]

Millar was almost certainly one of the last people to see Ryan and Ellingworth alive. Many sources state that the building was a warehouse, but Mr A.W. Snow, a paperboy in Dagenham at the time who lived in Oval Road North, has confirmed that the mine fell on a row of houses.[24] Millar states that there were no warehouses in Oval Road North, and that the parachute was dangling from the pointed roof of a house, level with the first-floor bedroom and about 2ft from the floor.[25]

The way in which the mine was hanging precariously made its fuse dangerously unstable and very difficult to work on. The area was cordoned off and inhabitants were evacuated to a nearby special school.[26] No doubt Ryan and Ellingworth were working out how to approach the task of defusing it when it suddenly exploded. Both were killed instantly. The blast was huge – a photograph published in the *Barking and Dagenham Recorder* shows houses on the other side of the road with their fronts completely blown in. The house where the mine had been hanging was completely destroyed, and all of the houses for several hundred yards had suffered severe damage.[27] Parachute mines routinely caused more damage than conventional bombs, as their slow descent prevented them from burrowing into the ground, and as a result the blast was not absorbed by the surrounding earth.[28]

Commander Moore and his assistant heard the blast just as they had finished work on their mine in New Road. Moore later told how he was the first person to see Ryan and Ellingworth's bodies and even though Ellingworth had been in close proximity to the mine when it exploded, he 'had a proper smile on his face' and Moore was quite sure that he had died a happy man.[29]

On 24 September 1940 – by coincidence the very same day that the George Cross was instituted as an award for actions which are not in the face of the enemy – Ellingworth's death was announced in the *Portsmouth Evening News*.[30] The notice from his wife read:

… On the 21st of September, very suddenly whilst serving his country, Reginald Vincent, C.P.O., R.N., H.M.S. Vernon, my devoted husband and best of dads, passed away … Duty nobly done, dear. A blow too deep for words.

There were also a number of tributes from other friends and family:

… In memory of Reg, died Sept. 21st. One of the best. Gone on his last commission – Kath and Fred.

… To the memory of Reg, a brave man who gave his life that others might live – Dick and Mrs Salter.

In loving memory of dear Reg, so suddenly taken from us, age 42. Deeply regretted by his loving mother-in-law A.E. Phillips, of Strode Road, and his brothers-in-law, all serving. His life given for others.

As a long-serving sailor who had made Portsmouth his home, Ellingworth's loss was obviously felt by many in the city who knew him. His widow's 'Thanks for Sympathy' notice in the *Evening News* on 4 October 1940 referred to the sentiments his death had been met with:

Mrs Ellingworth and family of 362 Copnor Road wish sincerely to thank all relatives, neighbours, friends of Powerscourt Road, Mr Privett of Copnor Road, for their great kindness, the Chaplains of H.M.S. Vernon and R.N. Barracks for their deep sympathy, the Captain and Commander of H.M.S. Vernon, the Commanding Officers of the mining school, the C.P.O.'s of the mess … and many friends of Reg's for their great kindness and sympathy to me, also for numerous letters and for beautiful floral tributes. I thank you, one and all. The day thou Gavest, Lord, is ended.[31]

For continual bravery in the face of danger over a prolonged period, both Ryan and Ellingworth were posthumously nominated for the George Cross. Many of the first awards of the George Cross were made to bomb disposal men who served during the Blitz of 1940 – ten out of the original twenty-four RMS men from HMS *Vernon* were awarded either the George Cross or the George Medal.[32] Reginald Ellingworth was buried in Milton Cemetery, Portsmouth, and his headstone bears the insignia of the George Cross.

Ellingworth's George Cross was announced in the *London Gazette* on 17 December 1940:

The King has been graciously pleased to approve the posthumous award of the George Cross, for great gallantry and undaunted devotion to duty, to Chief Petty Officer R.V. Ellingworth, R.N. C.P.O. Ellingworth, together with Lt. Cdr. Richard Ryan, R.N., went to a warehouse in Dagenham, Essex, where an unexploded bomb was hanging from a parachute. The pair, who had faced many dangers together, were both killed by its explosion and both were awarded the George Cross posthumously.[33]

It is interesting that Ellingworth's citation referred to an unexploded bomb rather than a mine. As already mentioned, official records show that the government was very anxious not to inform the Germans that naval parties were working on defusing their mines. As a result the press were prevented from making any mention of parachute mines. The people of Portsmouth read of Ellingworth's George Cross in the *Evening News* on 21 December 1940. The announcement referred simply to his 'gallantry and undaunted devotion to duty', and to the fact that no other information was available.[34] This lack of information reinforces just how dangerous the parachute mines were and how they were feared by the authorities.

The veil of secrecy over parachute mines continued for some time after the incident in Dagenham. In October 1940 the Admiralty and the Ministry of Home Security wanted to issue a statement regarding the destruction caused by parachute mines. It was blocked by the Air Ministry, on the grounds that not only would such a statement disclose the effects of the mines, but also that, in the words of one Air Ministry civil servant:

… it seems to be a bit odd to complain about 'wanton attacks', 'savagery' and 'barbarous weapons' and at the same time to minimise the extent of the damage which they have caused.[35]

Between them, Reg Ellingworth and Richard Ryan had saved hundreds if not thousands of lives during 1940, by not only defusing countless mines, but also capturing intact the first example of a 'C'-type parachute mine. HMS *Vernon* closed in 1996, and the site is now occupied by the Gunwharf Quays Development. Royal Navy Bomb Disposal still has a presence in Portsmouth, however, at Horsea Island.

Yet remarkably the story of Reg Ellingworth's George Cross did not end there. After the war in 1968 his medals were sold by his second wife Jessie for £720. Ellingworth's son Donald, himself a Dunkirk veteran, set about tracking them down, and eventually traced them to a collector in Canada. With £8,500 that he won on the pools in 1997, Donald Ellingworth bought back his father's medals, and immediately loaned them to the Imperial War Museum. Recovering the medals meant a great deal to Donald Ellingworth:

> With the loss of the medal, my father had been, to a certain extent, forgotten about … Tracing the medals was not easy, but I was determined not to give up.[36]

Reg Ellingworth's medals were unveiled in the Imperial War Museum's Victoria Cross and George Cross gallery on 28 May 1997.[37] The guest of honour, the Prince of Wales, greeted Donald Ellingworth with the memorable words, 'So you are the pools winner? Jolly good show – you spent the money well'.[38]

In 1998 Donald Ellingworth, who was 20 when his father was killed, visited the site in Oval Road North for the first time.[39] Reg Ellingworth has also been remembered in Dagenham Civic Centre, where a plaque was unveiled in 1999 in memory of him and other bomb disposal personnel killed in Dagenham during the Second World War.[40]

Reg Ellingworth's heroism showed an awe-inspiring level of calmness in the face of huge risk. To deal with unexploded mines continually, knowing the serious risks, called for a very special kind of bravery. It is impossible not to be incredibly moved by the work done by Ellingworth and his colleagues, and by his supreme sacrifice in order to save others. A long-serving sailor who had made Portsmouth his home, Ellingworth is a fine example of the best traditions of the Royal Navy and its men.

2

The Battleships: HMS *Royal Oak*, HMS *Hood* and HMS *Barham*

A S ONE OF the three main manning ports of the Royal Navy, Portsmouth provided the crews for much of the fleet during wartime. Thus, as many long-serving sailors settled in Portsmouth, a large proportion of crew members came from the city, or at least put down strong roots there. Inevitably, when ships were sunk the losses could be catastrophic. The amount of men lost in one single day whenever a battleship was sunk, for example, could be compared to the heavy losses suffered by the Pals battalions on the Western Front during the First World War. The impact on a strong naval community such as Portsmouth was keenly felt.

During wartime large warships rarely visited Portsmouth itself due to the increased risk of air attack.[1] The Home Fleet operated from its First World War anchorage at Scapa Flow in the Orkney Islands, while the Royal Navy also maintained significant fleets abroad. Three Portsmouth-crewed capital ships were sunk during the Second World War: HMS *Royal Oak*, HMS *Hood* and HMS *Barham*, resulting in the deaths of at least 218 sailors and Royal Marines from Portsmouth.

HMS *Royal Oak*, a Revenge-class battleship, was launched at Plymouth in 1914. She was commissioned into the Royal Navy in 1916, just in time to take part in the Battle of Jutland, and had just re-entered service in June 1939 after a refit. The *Royal Oak* weighed in at 33,500 tons fully laden, was over 600ft long and was armed with eight 15in guns in four turrets. She carried a crew of nearly 1,100 men. At 25 years old she was somewhat elderly, and although she had received upgrades throughout her life she had inadequate protection against torpedoes. She had been due to spend several years in the Mediterranean, but the onset of war meant that she joined the Home Fleet instead. She sailed from Portsmouth for the last time in August 1939. Many thought that she was a lucky ship – one author has described her as 'carrying Drake's Drum', a reference to the Spanish Armada of 1588.[2]

Among her crew in 1939 was 38-year-old Petty Officer Frederick Bealing.[3] Born in Gillingham, Dorset, Bealing joined the Royal Navy as a boy seaman in 1918. After initial training on board the training ship HMS *Powerful*, moored in Plymouth, Bealing then served

Frederick Bealing, pictured as a young seaman. *(Doris Bealing)*

on board the light cruisers HMS *Colombo*, HMS *Curacao* and HMS *Concord*, and the gunboat HMS *Bee*. He passed his tests for promotion to petty officer in 1921, at the extremely young age of 20. His daughter Doris recalled later that her father had left the navy prior to the Second World War to work for a Lord Nuttall on the Hampshire and Wiltshire border. When he was made redundant from his job on the Nuttall estate, he returned to Portsmouth and rejoined the navy when Doris was 6 months old.[4] Just prior to the start of the war he was promoted to regulating petty officer, one of the ship's 'policemen'.[5]

Although the Scapa Flow anchorage was seen as safer than the more southern naval ports, there was still much anxiety about the threat of U-boats breaching defences. During early October 1939, however, the *Royal Oak* was patrolling off the Orkney Islands, guarding against German surface raiders threatening to break into the Atlantic. After enduring a fierce storm, she arrived back at Scapa Flow on 11 October 1939. There she remained, her anti-aircraft guns adding to Scapa's shore defences.

Most of the *Royal Oak*'s crew 'turned in' early on the night of 13 October, resting after spending time at sea in rough weather. At 10.30 p.m., a last record was played over the ship's broadcast system. Colour Sergeant Harold Paice, 35 years old and from Cosham, was the senior marine non-commissioned officer on board. He stayed on watch until most men had gone to sleep before turning in for the night.[6]

Gunther Prien's *U-47* penetrated the defences of Scapa Flow on the night of 13/14 October, and identified the old battleship at anchor. After his first three torpedoes missed, Prien reloaded and attacked again. The first explosions were greeted with confusion on board the *Royal Oak* and reportedly the master-at-arms, the senior rating on board, ordered the crew to return to bed. Even fifteen minutes after the first torpedo struck many men were still asleep. The broadcast system had been knocked out, adding to the confusion, and as a result there was never a formal order to abandon ship.[7]

A fire on board quickly spread through the crowded mess decks, causing horrific casualties. It has been suggested that many more men were killed because the crew were not yet fully accustomed to war stations, and perhaps did not think themselves under threat in a supposedly safe anchorage. The historian Alexander McKee has also suggested that there was not enough lifesaving equipment on board.[8] Not all watertight hatches were closed. Once the gravity of the situation had been realised most men below decks had a maximum of five minutes to escape – not nearly enough time in dark, smoke-filled conditions. Marine Frederick Sandford, aged 31 and from Milton, tried to escape through an officer's bathroom and, finding it blocked,

Frederick Bealing (right) in tropical uniform as an older sailor. *(Doris Bealing)*

Anxious families read a list of men killed on the *Royal Oak*, posted outside the Royal Naval barracks in Portsmouth. *(The News 174)*

tried to open a door leading to an upper-deck gun battery. He was heard to shout 'we're done, it's stuck'.[9] He eventually got out on to the port side of the ship, but died there. Marine William Tuckwood, another Portsmouth man, was last seen selflessly helping another marine who had suffered horrific burns to his head.[10]

While the *Royal Oak* was sinking, *U-47* escaped, and Prien was later highly decorated by Hitler. Even Winston Churchill, then the First Lord of the Admiralty, described Prien's attack as a 'wonderful feat of arms'.[11] After the attack, huge stone causeways were built to block the route that *U-47* had taken into Scapa Flow.

Local small boats battled throughout the night to rescue survivors from the icy, oil-laden water, but despite their efforts 833 men were killed as a result of the sinking. Twenty-six of those who died are buried in Lyness Naval Cemetery, Orkney, including two men from Portsmouth – Petty Officer Edward Franckeiss, 30 and from Southsea, and Electrical Artificer Charles Benney, 37 and from Southwick. They are believed to have escaped the ship but drowned while awaiting rescue.[12] The rest of the men lost had no grave other than the sea, and most are remembered on the Portsmouth Naval Memorial. Sixty-six of those killed are known to have come from Portsmouth; many more will no doubt have had links with the city. Among the dead were Petty Officer Frederick Bealing, Colour Sergeant Harold Paice, Marine Frederick Sandford and Marine William Tuckwood. Over a hundred of those killed were boy seamen, under the age of 18 – the boys' mess deck was particularly badly hit, and many older seamen battled to try to rescue boys from the chaos.[13] The mother of one of the boys, Mrs Walker, had dreamt about the loss of the *Royal Oak*.[14] Her son, Boy First Class Cecil Walker, was 16 and from Cosham.

The Admiralty announced the loss of the *Royal Oak* early the next morning on 14 October 1939. BBC bulletins reported that there were at that time fifteen survivors, leading families to fear that there were only fifteen survivors in total. Later, lists of survivors were posted by the Admiralty at naval barracks and published in newspapers. Crowds gathered in Portsmouth at the HMS *Victory*[15] naval barracks and the Royal Marines barracks at Eastney to wait for news. Doris Bealing later recalled her experience after the *Royal Oak* was sunk:

> I remember going down to the barracks with my mother and there was a loudspeaker high up on the wall and we were waiting for the names of survivors to come through. With my friend we went up and down the street touching all the wooden window sills and saying, 'touch wood my daddy isn't dead'. Those are my most vivid memories, and I can remember my aunts being there and my mother crying, but they kept a lot of the sorrow from us as children … Well we were in a little room, that is all I can remember, with this loudspeaker. It seemed high on the wall to me, as a child. It was just the names coming out and you were hoping all the time that you would hear your father's name.[16]

The loss of so many Royal Marines from Portsmouth was greeted with the *Portsmouth Evening News* headline 'Eastney in mourning'.[17] A news reporter walked the streets of Eastney, and found small groups of women quietly talking to each other, unable to concentrate on anything else.

Countless families received a formal telegram from the Admiralty informing them that their husband or son was 'missing presumed killed', followed by confirmation of their fate, and a letter expressing the king and queen's sympathy. Iris Harris lived in an area where many sailors' wives received the fateful telegram from the Admiralty:

> I remember when she had the baby, I think he was a fortnight/three weeks old and I can see this telegram boy now coming down the road and her husband was a Royal Marine and he was on The Royal Oak at Scapa Flow, the baby was fortnight/three weeks old, terrible …[18]

The coverage given by the *Evening News* demonstrates how keenly felt the loss of the *Royal Oak* was in Portsmouth. Coming early in the war, the sinking was one of the country's first major disasters of the conflict, and the manner of her sinking, in what was thought to be a safe anchorage, also shocked many.

The *Royal Oak* still rests in Scapa Flow, and is a designated war grave. Royal Navy divers regularly replace her White Ensign in tribute to the hundreds of men who still rest in her.

Although officially classed as a battlecruiser, HMS *Hood* was in fact much larger than her battleship contemporaries, with a length of 860ft and a fully laden weight of 46,680 tons, and she was launched at John Browns in Scotland in 1918. As a battlecruiser, excessive armour had been sacrificed to give her more speed. She had been designed before the lessons of the Battle of Jutland, where several battlecruisers had been blown up by direct hits.

The main gate to Portsmouth Dockyard, a familiar sight to thousands of Portsmouth sailors throughout the years. *(Author)*

In the interwar years, the *Hood* represented British sea power around the world, and for many years she was the largest warship afloat.[19] She served as a floating ambassador, visiting many far-flung ports. This active role meant that she did not receive a much-needed major refit, although she received a succession of minor modifications throughout her life.[20] In fact, one author has even suggested that the *Hood* was scheduled to be scrapped in 1941, before the Second World War intervened.[21]

Upon the outbreak of war in 1939 HMS *Hood* was part of the Home Fleet, but in June 1940 she was hastily transferred to Gibraltar to join Force H. Whilst stationed in the Mediterranean, she took part in the bombardment of the French fleet at Mers-el-Kebir, before returning to Scapa Flow in August, where she was kept as a deterrent to prevent the German fleet breaking out into the Atlantic.[22] Although most of her crew were long-serving sailors, a number of new non-regular recruits had joined in the first two years of the war.[23] These new men were learning on the job. Despite this, it was commonly thought in 1941 that the *Hood*'s gunnery skills were second to none in the Royal Navy.[24]

In May 1941 the new German battleship *Bismarck* broke out into the North Sea, accompanied by the cruiser *Prinz Eugen*. The two ships represented a serious threat to British shipping, and the commander-in-chief of the Home Fleet, Admiral Sir Jack Tovey, despatched the *Hood* and the brand-new battleship *Prince of Wales* to intercept them. Tovey guessed correctly that the German ships would attempt to break into the Atlantic via the Denmark Strait separating

Greenland and Iceland, and sent the *Hood* and *Prince of Wales* in that direction. The *Hood* left Scapa Flow at 12.52 a.m. on 22 May.[25]

At 12.15 a.m. on 24 May, Vice-Admiral Lancelot Holland, based on the *Hood*, gave the order to 'prepare for action'. The rest of the Home Fleet was hours away. The ship's company (all officers, NCOs and enlisted personnel) were clothed in clean underwear – to prevent infection if they were wounded – duffle coat, waterproofs, lifebelts, steel helmet and anti-flash protection.[26] The enemy ships were sighted at 5.37 a.m., having been shadowed by British cruisers since the day before. The *Bismarck* fired her first salvo at 5.52 a.m., at a range of 25,000 yards. The first shots missed, but showered the *Hood* in foam. The third salvo hit and caused an ammunition fire on the boat deck, but it was not thought to be serious.[27] According to the reports of one survivor, the gunner's mate, Petty Officer Edward Bishop, 44 and from Portsmouth, ordered everyone clear of the fire.[28]

Whilst the fourth salvo missed, the fifth scored a direct hit at a range of 16,500 yards. It is believed that a 4in magazine was ignited, which in turn exploded the main 15in shell magazine. A lack of deck armour gave her little protection. Eyewitnesses on the *Prince of Wales* saw a pillar of fire 1,000ft high as the *Hood* exploded. The *Prince of Wales* withdrew, her guns defective. Many of her crew were lost when she was sunk off Singapore only months later.

Only three men were to survive of the *Hood*'s 1,418 crew. More might have lived had the shock of the icy cold water not prevented them from inflating their lifebelts. Many must have died of hypothermia. At least ninety-eight of those killed are known to have come from Portsmouth, of whom thirteen were Royal Marines. As so few of the crew survived, we have few accounts of what happened to the ship or its crew in her final moments. The loss of the *Hood* was announced by the Admiralty at 9 a.m. on 24 May 1941. The sinking of the Royal Navy's largest warship, and such a visible sign of British sea power, was met with a reaction out of proportion to the loss of the ship herself.[29]

In Portsmouth the loss of the *Hood* was marked by the *Evening News* in a much less dramatic fashion compared to that of the *Royal Oak*. This was perhaps due to the fact that she was

HMS *Hood*, photographed in 1940. *(Michael Mason/HMS* Hood *Association)*

HMS *Barham* explodes as her 15in shell magazine ignites. *(Imperial War Museum FLM/1984)*

lost several years into the war and people were more accustomed to losses, and that she was sunk in action by the *Bismarck* rather than torpedoed at anchor, as in the case of the *Royal Oak*. Nevertheless, the pages of the newspaper were filled with notices from the families of lost sailors and marines. The Buck family suffered an even heavier loss than most. Brothers Petty Officer Stoker Herbert Buck, 29 years old, and Mechanician Second Class Arthur Buck, 32 years old, were both killed on the *Hood*. Their parents, Samuel and Beatrice Buck, would have received not one but two telegrams from the Admiralty.

Leslie Matthews was a Royal Marine who had served on the *Hood* early in the war as an admiral's orderly. He was promoted to corporal in 1941, and as the *Hood* already had enough marine corporals he was transferred off the ship just before she set sail on her final voyage. He lost many friends on the *Hood*:

> It's such, such a vast ship, you know, a huge ship, to think that she would sink like that ... You never know your luck do you? But ... that's what happened ... so I don't meet any of them because they all sunk I mean, after that, they disappeared.[30]

HMS *Barham* was a Queen Elizabeth-class battleship, launched in 1914. She was named after Lord Barham, a First Lord of the Admiralty during the Napoleonic Wars. Weighing in at 33,000 tons fully laden, *Barham* was 643ft long, had a crew of 1,184, and was armed with eight 15in guns in four turrets. She joined the fleet in time to serve during the First World

War, seeing action at Jutland. Although she was hit in the battle, she escaped serious damage. Twenty-six men were killed, however, and thirty-seven wounded.[31]

Barham served in the Mediterranean for much of the interwar period. She became known as 'the Beery Barham', for having a drinking culture, although this was not untypical of many Royal Navy warships of the time. She was also known as a good sporting ship, her sports teams winning many honours.

The Queen Elizabeth-class ships were approaching obsolescence at the start of the Second World War, but given the lack of battleships constructed during the interwar period they were pressed into service nonetheless. She had actually been decommissioned at Portsmouth in February 1938, but sailed for the Mediterranean in June 1938 after minor modifications. Like the *Royal Oak*, however, she boasted little in the way of defence against torpedoes.

Although she began the war in the Mediterranean, *Barham* was sent to reinforce the Home Fleet and carried out patrols in the North Sea. Four men were killed in a little-known incident on 28 December 1939, when she was hit by a torpedo from *U-30*, which tore a hole in the ship 32ft wide and 6ft deep. She went to Liverpool for repairs, before sailing again in April 1940.

In August 1940 *Barham* sailed again for the Mediterranean. She served for the rest of 1940 and early 1941 with the Mediterranean fleet, commanded by Admiral Sir Andrew Cunningham. In May 1941 she was the target of an air raid, which killed three, mortally wounded two and wounded six others. One of those killed was Chief Petty Officer Albert Hall from Portsmouth. Requiring major repairs, the *Barham* sailed for Durban in South Africa via the Suez Canal, after which she returned to the Mediterranean.

The naval war in the Mediterranean was closely linked to the fighting in North Africa, and a new offensive was planned to take place in the Western Desert on 18 November 1941. Admiral Cunningham put to sea in order to support the attack, giving fire support and intercepting Axis shipping convoys.

German U-boats had recently been sent to the Mediterranean to reinforce their Italian allies. *U-331* was lurking off the North African coast, and on 25 November 1941 managed to reach the British fleet undetected, despite a sizeable screen of destroyers and the fleet using zigzagging tactics to present a more difficult target to submarines. The U-boat's commander, Freiherr Hans-Diedrich von Tiesenhausen, successfully fired a salvo of three torpedoes at the *Barham*.

Survivors reported four explosions taking place in less than three seconds and the explosion of *Barham*'s magazine provided some of the most dramatic images of the war at sea. Although the *Royal Oak* and the *Hood* had also suffered similar explosions, that so many other ships were close at hand to witness it made the disaster all the more startling. She remains the only battleship to have been sunk at sea by a U-boat.[32] Admiral Cunningham described witnessing the sinking of the *Barham* as 'a horrible and awe-inspiring spectacle when one realised what it meant'.[33]

A total of 861 men were lost in the sinking of the *Barham*, with fifty-four of them from Portsmouth. Petty Officer Edward Usmar, 35 and from Southsea, went down on the *Barham*. His brother, Petty Officer Harry Usmar, 39, had been killed on the *Royal Oak*. Another sailor on board the *Barham* was 19-year-old Ordinary Seaman Ray Green, from North End. His family believe that the *Barham* was his first and only ship. Ray's brother Doug, a flight sergeant pilot, had been killed on 15 April 1941 when his Lockheed Hudson Coastal Command aircraft crashed.[34]

Portsmouth Naval Memorial on Southsea Common. The memorial records the names of 14,896 Portsmouth-based sailors lost during the Second World War who have no known grave other than the sea. *(Author)*

The loss of the *Barham* was concealed from the world until 27 January 1942, and *The Times* finally published a casualty list on 23 February 1942. The Admiralty believed that the Germans had not known the *Barham*'s identity nor that she had sunk, and hoped that by concealing her loss they might misinform German intelligence. This contrasts with the *Royal Oak* and the *Hood*, the losses of which were announced almost immediately.

There is also an intriguing postscript to the *Barham* story. In November 1941 a medium, Helen Duncan, held a séance in Portsmouth, where she indicated knowledge that HMS *Barham* had been sunk. Reportedly she summoned the spirit of a dead sailor, wearing a *Barham* cap tally, who announced 'my ship is sunk'.[35] The sinking had only been revealed to relatives of the crew, and was only officially announced in January 1942 due to concerns over the impact on morale. In 1942 Helen Duncan was arrested and tried under the Witchcraft Act of 1735, and jailed for nine months. Even Winston Churchill described Duncan's trial and imprisonment as 'tomfoolery'.[36]

The loss of three battleships full of local men took a heavy toll on the people of Portsmouth. Like the losses experienced at Jutland in 1916, there can have been very few people in Portsmouth who had not either lost a family member on the *Royal Oak*, the *Hood* or *Barham*, or did not know of a friend or former colleague who had been killed on one of the battleships.

3

Portsmouth's Boy Sailors

MANY WILL BE familiar with the tragic stories of 16- and 17-year-old boys who lied about their age to serve during the First World War. Not only was it much easier for somebody to lie about their age in 1914, but many recruiters willingly turned a blind eye. After the slaughter on the Western Front, however, the requirements to prove age became more stringent. The death of so many boys in action was not good for morale, either at home or on the front line.[1] During the Second World War, only one Portsmouth soldier died under the age of 18.[2]

Yet the Royal Navy had been recruiting and employing 'underage' sailors for hundreds of years. Boy Jack Cornwell, the youngest ever winner of the Victoria Cross, was aged just 17 when he was mortally wounded at Jutland in 1916. Whilst Cornwell's Victoria Cross was celebrated, the fact that he was at sea fighting was not thought at all remarkable at the time.[3] Only relatively recently in British history had all young people been able to receive education provided by the state, and in any case most boys and girls left school much earlier than the present leaving age of 16. Historically, a boy might be apprenticed to a master at 14 in order to learn a trade, and so, against the background of the time, boys joining the Royal Navy and serving at sea does not appear as startling as it first appears.

Further back in history, the Nelsonian Royal Navy had made ample use of boys as 'powder monkeys', carrying bags of gunpowder from the ship's hold to the gun crews. Nelson himself had joined as a young boy to serve as an 'officer's servant'.[4] Boys joined at such a young age in order to 'learn the ropes' – literally in the case of seamen in the pre-steam era.[5] This approach, whilst it might seem harsh from a modern perspective, paid dividends with the professionalism that it engendered. Indeed, it is noticeable that many of the older Portsmouth sailors mentioned elsewhere in this book began their career as boy seamen, men such as Reg Ellingworth and Henry Miller. Both had joined the Royal Navy whilst boys, both at HMS *Impregnable* in Plymouth, both served in submarines during their career[6] and both were awarded the George Cross posthumously.[7]

Officers also joined at a relatively young age – William Hussey, for example, entered Britannia Royal Naval College at the age of 14.[8] Officers in particular were expected to spend a lifetime in the service if they progressed up the promotion ladder, unlike ratings who usually served a maximum of twenty-two years. Joining so young meant that they could begin their education and training early during their formative years.[9]

All boy seamen entered training hulks for the first few years of their service. These hulks included HMS *St Vincent* in Portsmouth and HMS *Impregnable* in Plymouth; warships that had long since retired from active service. The boys were awoken at 6 a.m., and would scrub the deck until breakfast at 8 a.m. After prayers they would attend lessons until tea at 5 p.m. After a daily inspection they would be dismissed at 6 p.m., at which point they would finally have time to themselves.[10] If their existence seems tough seen through modern eyes, it was only to harden them to the rigours of life at sea at a time when sailors were still very much performing physical labour.

Once boys had finished their training, they would be posted to a ship. For many this would be one of the Royal Navy's battleships, where boys were accommodated in their own mess. The treatment of boys varied from ship to ship. Some did experience bullying and cruelty, but other ships could have kinder crew. The boy seaman was at the bottom of the ladder, having to call even an able seaman 'sir'. They were not even allowed to talk to older ratings unless they were working together.[11] They were also paid very poorly, and were not allowed the daily rum ration whilst underage. Even after they had joined a ship at sea, boy seamen spent half of their day in classes with the ship's schoolmaster.[12]

Once at sea on active service, boy seamen faced exactly the same risks as anybody else serving on a warship. Ten boy seamen from Portsmouth were killed during the Second World War, and perhaps the saddest statistic is that five of the boy seamen were killed whilst serving on HMS *Royal Oak*: Boy First Class Gordon Ogden, 16 and from Milton; Boy First Class Robert Spalding, 16 and from Milton; Boy First Class Cecil Walker, 16 and from Cosham; Signal Boy Charles Eyres, 17; and Boy First Class Lesley Jelley, 17 and from Milton.

It is believed that so many boy seamen were serving on board the *Royal Oak* because she was in a – supposedly – safe theatre of war, and there was thought to be little risk of them coming to any harm. The boys' mess deck on the *Royal Oak* was particularly badly hit. As so few of her boy seamen survived, accounts of what exactly happened are few and far between. It is believed that some older crew members battled to save the boys and evacuate them through a manhole.[13] All of the *Royal Oak* boy seamen who were lost have no known grave other than the sea, and are remembered on the Portsmouth Naval Memorial.

Immediately after the *Royal Oak* disaster, the then First Lord of the Admiralty Winston Churchill was questioned by MPs over the policy of sending boys to sea.[14] There were also calls to withdraw personnel under 18 from active service until they had come of age. Churchill replied that just under 5,000 boys under 18 were serving in the Royal Navy, that entry at a young age was important for training for a life at sea, and that the consent of parents was always required. The sterling performance of ex-boy seamen such as Reg Ellingworth and Henry Miller certainly supports Churchill's statement regarding the importance and usefulness of boys entering the service early in life. Confusion was also caused by the War Office's pledge not to send younger soldiers overseas on active service with the army, with many interpreting this undertaking as including the Royal Navy. The Admiralty had to repeatedly stress the difference between service on land and at sea.[15] Nonetheless, many anxious parents wrote to the Admiralty requesting that their sons be sent back to shore.

Even though boy seamen continued to go to sea after the *Royal Oak* disaster, the Admiralty was extremely careful to limit the number of young sailors on board ships, particularly on active operations. Only in exceptional circumstances – and with their parents' permission – were boys under 17 allowed to go to sea.[16] When HMS *Hood* was sunk by the *Bismarck* in 1941, only two boy seamen from Portsmouth were killed: Boy First Class Jack Goff, 17; and Boy First Class Leslie Joyce, 17 and from Mile End. Both Goff and Joyce are remembered on the Portsmouth Naval Memorial. The *Hood* was a larger ship than the *Royal Oak* and all but three of her crew were lost. This suggests that the Admiralty had significantly cut the number of boy seamen on board by 1941.

Boy First Class Jack Lamb, 16 and from Kingston, was serving on board HMS *Dunedin* after the supposed ban on 16-year-olds serving at sea. Either Lamb's parents had given permission for him to remain at sea, or there had been no opportunity to return him to shore. The *Dunedin*, a light cruiser, was attacked and sunk by *U-124* on 24 November 1941. Lamb is remembered on the Portsmouth Naval Memorial, one of twenty-six Portsmouth sailors to be killed out of a total of 420 dead.[17]

Some boys joined the Royal Navy through routes other than the training hulks. Boys who were destined for a career as either electrical or engine room artificers also joined the Royal Navy at a young age, but spent up to five years training as apprentices in Royal Dockyard schools. Boys who entered the dockyard schools for technical training were among the most gifted young men joining the Royal Navy.[18] Apprentice Electrical Artificer George Garnham, 17 and from North End, died on 4 February 1941 and is buried in Milton Cemetery. Apprentice Electrical Artificer Raymond Whitehorn, 16 and from Southsea, was serving at HMS *Raleigh*, a shore base, when he died on 14 September 1946, after the end of hostilities. He is buried in Kingston Cemetery, Portsmouth.

After completing their initial training, young officers served as midshipmen, and one midshipman from Portsmouth was killed in 1941 at the age of just 17. Arthur Jay, from Southsea, was on board HMS *Neptune*, a cruiser, when she was sunk by a mine in the Mediterranean on 19 December 1941. Midshipman Jay is remembered on the Plymouth Naval Memorial. Only one man survived out of a crew of 764 – four of whom came from Portsmouth.[19] Very few midshipmen were killed during the war as they were usually promoted very quickly to the rank of sub-lieutenant, unlike during peacetime when they had to wait at least eighteen months before being promoted.[20]

Society had reviled against underage boys serving in the army, largely due to the losses of many 16- and 17-year-olds on the Western Front in the Great War. The army had made its checks on age more stringent, and only one underage soldier from Portsmouth died in the Second World War, but underage service was still seen as the norm for the Royal Navy, and would be for some years afterwards.

4

'Most promising, should go far': Lieutenant Commander William Hussey DSO, DSC

UPON THE OUTBREAK of war in September 1939, the Royal Navy was still the largest force sailing the world's oceans. Imbued with the legacy of legendary figures such as Rodney, Nelson and Fisher, some of the most daring officers of the Second World War were the Royal Navy's destroyer captains. In 1940 Lieutenant Commander Gerard Roope, commander of HMS *Glowworm*, rammed the German heavy cruiser *Admiral Hipper*. *Glowworm* sank, and Roope was drowned, but the *Hipper* was heavily damaged, and Roope was posthumously awarded the Victoria Cross. Lord Louis Mountbatten also became famous for his exploits in command of HMS *Kelly* and the 5th Destroyer Flotilla, immortalised in the film *In Which We Serve*.

Portsmouth's most prominent naval commander killed during the Second World War was an officer in very much the same mould: Lieutenant Commander William Hussey, who was also Portsmouth's most highly decorated sailor to be killed between 1939 and 1945. His career shows how long years of training and education went into forming the Royal Navy's seagoing junior commanders of the Second World War.

William Frederick Eyre Hussey was born in Cheltenham on 7 November 1908, the son of Frederick Kinnear Eyre Hussey and his wife Edith Mary.[1] Hussey entered the Royal Navy as an officer cadet on 15 May 1922, at the age of 13. After almost four years at the Royal Naval College, Dartmouth, Hussey was posted to the battleship HMS *Royal Oak* as a cadet midshipman on 6 January 1926. On 15 September he was rated as a full midshipman.

On 1 November 1926 Hussey was transferred to the light cruiser HMS *Emerald*, remaining on board for almost a year and a half until 3 April 1928, when he was transferred to the *Emerald*'s sister ship, HMS *Enterprise*. On 1 January 1929 William Hussey was promoted to acting sub-lieutenant. Two days later he left HMS *Enterprise* and was posted to undertake a course at the Royal Naval College, Greenwich. Less than a month after enrolling at Greenwich, Hussey received a glowing report from his commanding officer, Captain Pridham-Wippell:

Exceptional … most promising, should go far. Leadership excellent for his age, possesses tact and personality and will acquire more self-confidence with experience. Physical qualities very good indeed.[2]

Having such a glowing report on his service record no doubt gave William Hussey the prospect of a promising career in the Royal Navy – he had already been marked out as having great potential. Whilst at Greenwich he also passed a certificate in French. On a slightly different note, he spent three weeks in hospital at Chatham with rubella in late February, and in August he spent ten days in hospital at Plymouth with tonsillitis. Despite these minor setbacks, on 1 August 1929 he was promoted to the rank of sub-lieutenant.

After leaving Greenwich, Hussey was posted to HMS *Dolphin*, the Royal Navy's submarine depot in Gosport, as an additional submarine officer on 5 May 1930. After a short posting at *Dolphin*, Hussey was posted to the depot ship HMS *Medway* on 1 September 1930 as an additional spare gunnery officer, and there awaited a posting to a submarine. On 1 December he finally joined the submarine HMS *Osiris*.

Whilst on board HMS *Osiris*, William Hussey took his exams for promotion to lieutenant. He was evidently successful, for on 5 November 1930 his commanding officer, Captain G. Arbuthnot, recommended him for promotion. On the same date Hussey was granted his watchkeeping certificate, and was subsequently promoted to lieutenant on 1 May 1931. This promotion was a significant step for any naval officer towards commanding his own ship in the future. At the age of 22, Hussey was also relatively young for a lieutenant.

In 1932 tragedy struck when Hussey's mother Edith died at the age of 54. On a happier note, less than a year later in September 1933, William Hussey married Diana Andrews in Marylebone, London.[3] For several months during 1933 Hussey was ashore without a posting, until he joined the battleship HMS *Iron Duke* on 10 October 1933.[4] The *Iron Duke* had been Admiral Jellicoe's flagship at Jutland in 1916, and had been converted to become a gunnery training ship in the 1930s. After a year on the *Iron Duke* Hussey was transferred to the submarine minelayer HMS *Sealion*, then under construction at Cammell Laird in Birkenhead.[5] The next few years of his career were spent on submarines, including a spell on board HMS *Cyclops*, the depot ship of the 1st Submarine Flotilla in the Mediterranean.[6]

After another short spell ashore, Hussey returned to surface vessels and was posted to the destroyer HMS *Wakeful*, part of the Home Fleet, in February 1936.[7] In April he was appointed the senior naval officer on the destroyer HMS *Hero*, still under construction at Vickers-Armstrong in Newcastle. *Hero* was commissioned in October 1936, after a more senior officer had been appointed to command the ship. Hussey remained on *Hero* as a lieutenant, however, and she sailed to join the 2nd Destroyer Flotilla in the Mediterranean.[8]

After serving eight years as a lieutenant, William Hussey was promoted to lieutenant commander on 1 May 1939, and on 31 July 1939 was given command of HMS *Vesper*, a destroyer that had been launched in 1917. After being put into reserve some years before, the *Vesper* was re-activated in 1937 and was in the process of rejoining the fleet.

Although the early months of the Second World War are often known as the 'phoney war', the Royal Navy went into action almost immediately. For the first few months of the war HMS *Vesper* was deployed on convoy escort duties and anti-submarine patrols in the English Channel and the South-west Approaches. An ex-submarine officer, Hussey found himself in the position of 'poacher-turned-gamekeeper'. It was obviously a role that he excelled at, and Hussey was awarded the Distinguished Service Cross (DSC) for 'successful action against enemy submarines'. Hussey's DSC was announced in the *London Gazette* on 23 December 1939.[9] Between January and April 1940 the *Vesper* escorted convoys in the Channel and the North Sea. With the British Expeditionary Force (BEF) withdrawing to Dunkirk, HMS *Vesper* was ordered to Harwich to support the evacuation. On 10 May the *Vesper* embarked a demolition party, and set sail for Ymuiden in Holland for the hazardous duty of destroying oil storage tanks.[10] From there, on 13 May, *Vesper* assisted with the evacuation of Dutch officials from the Hook of Holland. During June she was deployed to Dover with the 19th Flotilla to provide naval gunfire support for the BEF at Treport. In all cases Hussey took the *Vesper* into the direction of the enemy, and for these actions Hussey was Mentioned in Despatches.[11]

During July and August, when Britain was under threat of invasion, HMS *Vesper* joined the 21st Flotilla at Sheerness, and performed anti-invasion and escort duties in the Channel and North Sea. During September she deployed with the destroyers HMS *Garth* and HMS *Campbell* for a patrol off the Dutch coast. A planned bombardment of the German invasion fleet at Ostend was cancelled, however, due to bad weather. October and November brought more convoy escort duties, while on 8 October *Vesper* towed the damaged escort destroyer HMS *Hambledon* to Sheerness after she had struck a mine in the Thames Estuary.

In December 1940 HMS *Vesper* was transferred to the Western Approaches Command, and sailed to the Clyde. She began more convoy escort duties on 19 December, in company with the destroyers HMS *Harvester* and HMS *Highlander*, to escort convoy WS5A through the North-west Approaches. January and February 1941 brought more convoy escort duties from the Clyde.

In February, Lieutenant Commander Hussey left HMS *Vesper* after an eventful eighteen months in command, and was posted to take command of the brand-new destroyer HMS *Lively*. Bringing a new ship into service was to be yet another highlight of Hussey's career, and was no doubt a reward for his successful time in command of the *Vesper*. *Lively* had been launched in January 1941, and after trials she was commissioned for active service in July, crewed mainly by sailors from Devonport, Plymouth. On 30 July HMS *Lively* sailed to Scapa Flow to take on board stores, and in August she was ordered to join Western Approaches Command. After completing sea trials and training, or 'working up', with ships of the Home Fleet, on 22 August she was hurriedly despatched to assist a French minelaying submarine that had become damaged off the Norwegian Coast.[12]

Returning to Scapa Flow on 28 August, she sailed for Greenock to join a special escort group for convoy WS11, with the aircraft carrier HMS *Furious* taking Hurricane fighter-bombers to Malta. Arriving at Gibraltar on 10 September, HMS *Lively* joined the 4th Destroyer Flotilla, part of the famous Force H. During 1941 the Royal Navy was making strenuous efforts to reinforce the crucial island of Malta, and HMS *Lively* escorted HMS *Furious* and HMS *Ark Royal* to deliver aircraft to the beleaguered isle. The ships forming Operation Halberd sailed from Gibraltar on 24 September, and were also escorted by the battleships *Rodney*, *Nelson* and *Prince of Wales*. During Operation Halberd, *Lively* also came under air attack for the first time. Several days later, on 30 September, she was also attacked by the Italian submarine *Adua*, which was sunk by depth charges, and carried out anti-submarine operations with her sister ship, HMS *Legion*.

HMS *Lively* underway in Grand Harbour, Valetta, in Malta, November 1941. *(Imperial War Museum GM/165)*

HMS *Lively* returned to Gibraltar on 1 October. On 14 October she was detached from Force H and transferred to Malta. After arriving on 21 October she joined Force K, a special group formed for attacking enemy shipping in the central Mediterranean. On the night of 8 November the group sailed to intercept a convoy that had been disclosed by intercepted Italian signals – the next day Force K encountered the convoy, and HMS *Lively* fired upon the transport ship *Duisburg* and then the Italian destroyer *Euro*. The convoy and its escort were caught unawares and could barely reply. By the time the British destroyers withdrew at 2 a.m., all of the transports had been sunk, one Italian destroyer was sunk and two were seriously damaged. The only damage to HMS *Lively* was splinters from a shell which burst overhead and holed the funnel. The wiping out of the convoy cut the supplies reaching the Axis forces in North Africa by 50 per cent, resulting in the Italians temporarily suspending convoys across the Mediterranean. In February 1942 Hussey was awarded the Distinguished Service Order (DSO) for the attack on the Italian convoy.[13]

Several weeks later, on 24 November, Force K sailed to intercept another convoy, and the next day HMS *Lively* sank two German tankers, dodging the escorting destroyers and an air escort of Stukas. She then returned to Malta for repairs. A grateful Winston Churchill sent Force K a congratulatory message:

> Many congratulations on your fine work since you arrived at Malta, and will you please tell all ranks and ratings from me that the two exploits in which they have been engaged, namely the annihilation of the enemy's convoys on 9/11 and of the two oil ships on Monday last, have played a very definite part in the great battle now raging in Libya. The work of the Force has been most fruitful and all concerned may be proud to have been a real help to Britain and our cause.[14]

After leaving Malta, HMS *Lively* escorted HMS *Breconshire* to Alexandria. Following an uneventful journey she returned to Malta, and from there sailed again with Force K on 18 December 1941. From then on HMS *Lively*'s war moved to the North African theatre. On 19 December Force K ran into an Italian minefield off Tripoli, and HMS *Neptune* and HMS *Kandahar* were sunk. According to reports, Hussey pleaded to be allowed to remain and pick up survivors, but was ordered to retire. At one point he even attempted to take the *Lively* alongside the *Kandahar*. Hussey gave evidence at the inquiry into the *Neptune* and *Kandahar* sinkings, stating that he had not seen anything untoward prior to the *Neptune* going down.[15]

Returning to Malta the next day, HMS *Lively* enjoyed a welcome Christmas in Malta before spending the next few months escorting convoys to and from the beleaguered island. On 14 February 1942, HMS *Lively* was escorting a convoy between Malta and Alexandria when the convoy was attacked by Axis aircraft. The merchant ship SS *Rowallan Castle* was heavily damaged and later sank, despite attempts by *Lively* to tow her to safety. After an uneventful few weeks, on 11 March 1942 HMS *Lively* rescued survivors from the sinking of HMS *Naiad*.

HMS *Lively* was involved in another major action on 22 March 1941, which became known as the Second Battle of Sirte. While escorting a convoy, Force K encountered a vastly superior fleet of Italian battleships and cruisers. After a smokescreen had been laid, HMS *Lively* launched a torpedo attack, along with the cruisers *Sikh*, *Hero* and *Havock*. HMS *Lively* was hit by splinters from a 15in shell, which burst alongside, and although she suffered some flooding, she continued to fight. At one point *Lively* was hammering away at the giant Italian flagship *Littorio*, which should, on paper, have blown the *Lively* out of the water.[16] She was forced to withdraw after a near miss, and was still under air attack the next day, suffering more damage. She detached from the fleet and sailed to Tobruk for repairs. Although damaged, the *Lively* had helped to prevent the destruction of the convoy, which escaped unharmed.

By April 1942 the *Lively* had been repaired and was able to sail for Alexandria to rejoin the flotilla. April and May 1942 saw the *Lively* deployed off the North African coast on support, interception and screening duties. On 10 May HMS *Lively* deployed with the destroyers *Jervis*, *Jackal* and *Kipling* to intercept a convoy sailing between Crete and Benghazi. The ships were specifically warned to retire if sighted by aircraft, as they could expect only limited air support. It was a very dangerous mission – one historian, in fact, has referred to it as a 'suicide mission'.[17]

The next day however, the reporting station at Alexandria warned the force that an air attack, coming from the occupied island of Crete, was imminent.[18] The captain, leading the flotilla on board HMS *Jervis*, duly ordered a return to the relative safety of Alexandria. Soon after, however, HMS *Lively* came under heavy and sustained dive-bombing attacks 100 miles north-east of Tobruk. One Stuka dropped four bombs on her, virtually unopposed. At least three of the bombs struck the forecastle, passing through three decks before detonating and ripping out the front of the ship. Due to her speed, the ship's bow drove straight into the sea. She sank very quickly with heavy loss of life. Seventy-six of the ship's company were killed or missing.

Men who had been on the bridge were scattered over a large area by the explosions. Hussey, however, was seen floating calmly off of the bridge into the water, but then became separated from the rest of the crew. He was seen waving by the crew of HMS *Jervis*, and was encouraged with a loud-hailer while the surviving destroyer sailed to pluck him out of the sea.[19] Hussey was duly hauled on board the *Jervis*, but sadly died of his wounds during the night, despite the medical officer attempting artificial respiration.[20] In keeping with naval tradition he was buried at sea, and is remembered on the Plymouth Naval Memorial. As HMS *Lively* was mainly manned by crew from Devonport, Hussey was the only casualty from Portsmouth. William Hussey was posthumously Mentioned in Despatches, adding a final award to an already impressive fighting record.[21] Although Hussey had been warned to retire if sighted by aircraft, the fact that he was afterwards Mentioned in Despatches suggests that his superiors were not unhappy with his conduct in exposing *Lively* to attack.

The image of a destroyer captain valiantly taking his ship into action with the enemy, with little air cover and under grave threat of attack, is extremely stirring indeed. Such an action was in the finest traditions of the Royal Navy and its captains. One only has to look at the actions of more modern naval commanders to see how the deeds of men such as William Hussey played an important part in perpetuating the culture of the Royal Navy. In the Falklands War in 1982, Captain David Hart-Dyke took HMS *Coventry* – a Portsmouth-based ship – into the line of fire again and again, until she was eventually overwhelmed and sunk by air attack in a manner very similar to that of HMS *Lively*.

During his brief war service, William Hussey had commanded his ships with great skill and bravery, and such was the spirit imbued in naval officers from a very young age – that one day they might have to sacrifice themselves and their ship in the face of overwhelming odds.

5

Portsmouth's Submariners

SOON AFTER THE Royal Navy began operating submarines early in the twentieth century, HMS *Dolphin* in Gosport became Britain's principal submarine base. As a result, many Portsmouth sailors had close connections with the submarine service, and 112 Portsmouth men were killed serving on submarines during the Second World War.

From early on in its history, the Submarine Service developed a highly individual character all of its own, and due to the particular danger involved and the claustrophobic conditions, a strong brotherhood developed. In its early years, some conservative figures in the Royal Navy had even gone so far as to describe the submarine as underhand and un-British. Adopting this image, submariners took to flying the Jolly Roger when returning to port after a successful patrol. Serving on submarines also called for a particular kind of sailor, tolerant to the conditions. Hygiene was difficult due to privations on water supply, and a lack of space meant that the men virtually lived in each other's pockets. In the event of illness there was little chance of medical help beyond basic first aid. Many submarines did not carry a proper cook, meaning that other ratings took turns to attempt to cook instead.[1]

Serving in submarines was highly dangerous, and even in peacetime accidents frequently occurred. This danger was multiplied in wartime, when the abandonment of many peacetime safety precautions led to more accidents which, in submarines, had much more serious consequences. The general stresses of war also added to the strain and tiredness that bore heavily on many a submariner.[2] The causes of submarine losses are hard to prove – due to their *modus operandi* underwater and being frequently out of contact, they often disappeared without trace.[3] Often they simply failed to return to port on the planned date, and their fate was recorded starkly as 'missing, presumed lost'.[4] All submariners leaving port on a patrol would have been fully aware of these risks.

Service in submarines was also highly active, and it is no coincidence that many submariners were decorated for bravery. Whilst many people are well aware of the German U-boats that terrorised the North Atlantic, British submarines also played an active but lesser-known role

Able Seaman Henry Miller GC of
HMS *Unity. (RN Submarine Museum)*

in disrupting Axis trade, especially in the Mediterranean. In fact, taking into account the number of submarines lost in the Mediterranean, the decorations awarded and the amount of Axis shipping lost, the Mediterranean was for the British Submarine Service what the North Atlantic was to Doenitz's infamous wolf packs.

The first Royal Navy submarine to be lost in the Second World War, HMS *Oxley*, sank on 10 September 1939, only a matter of days after the outbreak of war. On board were Able Seaman John Banks, 31 and from Portsmouth, and Leading Seaman Percy Fairbrace, 31 and from Southsea. The *Oxley* was the first British naval loss of the war, and sadly was lost due to friendly fire from the submarine HMS *Triton*. The *Oxley* had strayed into the *Triton*'s patrol area in the North Sea and had not responded when challenged. The commanding officer had no option but to assume that the *Oxley* was a hostile vessel.[5] It was a stark lesson that crews had to sharpen their alertness and communications during wartime.

After the sinking of the *Oxley* the pattern of losses continued. During the early years of the war in particular, barely a month went by without a submarine being lost with Portsmouth men on board – *Seahorse, Thistle, Tarpon, Narwahl, Thames, H49* and *Syrtis* were lost in the North Sea. Once Italy entered the war in 1940 the Mediterranean became a crucial theatre, with control of the sea vital to the campaign in North Africa. *Grampus, Odin, Orpheus, Triad, Rainbow, Triton,*

Regulus, Undaunted, Union, P32, P33, Tetrarch, Perseus, Triumph, P38, Pandora, Upholder, Olympus, Utmost, Traveller, P48, P222, P311, Tigris, Thunderbolt, Regent, Parthian, Usurper, Trooper, Simoom and *Sickle* were all lost in the Mediterranean. Their role was so critical that German General Fritz Bayerlein, Chief of Staff of Rommel's Afrika Korps, remarked, 'we should have taken Alexandria and reached the Suez Canal if it had not been for the work of your submarines'.[6]

Comparatively fewer submarines were lost in the Atlantic – *Spearfish, H31* and *Unique*. Later in the war, after Italy surrendered and the war in the Mediterranean was won, submarines were transferred to the Far East, and *Stonehenge* and *Strategem* were lost in that theatre. *Swordfish* was lost in the English Channel, south of St Catherine's Point on the Isle of Wight. All of the submarines mentioned had at least one Portsmouth sailor on board; most had more.

One of the bravest acts by a Portsmouth submariner took place on board HMS *Unity*, which was lost on 29 April 1940. Able Seaman Henry Miller, 39 and from Southsea, was born in Poole in 1900 and joined the Royal Navy when he left school aged 15. Originally at HMS *Impregnable* in Plymouth and continuing his training at HMS *Ganges* in Suffolk, he was rated as an ordinary seaman and served on a succession of destroyers, cruisers and depot ships. The portion of his service record up until 1929 shows that he only served on surface ships, so Miller must have gained his 'dolphins' – the distinctive submariner's qualification badge worn on the left breast – relatively late in his naval career, some time in the 1930s.

On 29 April 1940 the *Unity* collided with the SS *Atle Jarl*, a Norwegian merchant ship, while leaving Blyth Harbour for a North Sea patrol.[7] The submarine was seriously damaged and began to sink. Lieutenant John Low went below to attend to the engine in order to buy some time for the crew to escape. When he called for somebody to assist him Able Seaman Miller volunteered:

> Knowing the submarine to be in immediate danger of sinking, and knowing that, in that event, they must be drowned by the sudden inrush of water … [Miller] deliberately went below to assist his lieutenant at a moment when he knew that any chance of regaining the deck was so infinitesimal as not to be worth even considering.[8]

One of Miller's shipmates, Engine Room Artificer Rob Roy McCurrach, remembered Miller, saying to him: 'I'll go Bob, I'm better placed.'[9] Miller was made a Military Member of the British Empire, which was announced in the *London Gazette* on 16 August 1940.[10] Miller's MBE was later exchanged for the new George Cross when the award was instituted later the same year. Miller became one of only two Portsmouth servicemen killed in the Second World War to receive a supreme award for bravery. Interestingly, the other – Chief Petty Officer Reg Ellingworth – had also served in submarines earlier in his career.

The heaviest losses of Portsmouth submariners were experienced on 12 January 1940 when six men were lost on board HMS *Seahorse*, and also on 20 October 1940 when six men were lost on board HMS *Triad*. The *Seahorse* was originally believed to have struck a mine in the Heligoland Bight off the west coast of Denmark, but is now thought to have been depth charged in error by British minesweepers.[11] Lost on board were Leading Stoker John Kewell, aged 25 and from Paulsgrove; Stoker First Class John Marshall, 29 and from Landport; Engine Room Artificer Leonard Wilson, aged 23 and from Southsea; Electrical Artificer Ernest Summers, aged 28; Warrant Engineer Alexander Cockburn, aged 33; and Engine Room Artificer Archibald

Smith, 25 and from Southsea. The *Triad* was sunk by gunfire and torpedo attack off Calabria, Italy, by the Italian submarine *Enrico Toti*.[12] On board were Engine Room Artificer William Dunstane, aged 24 and from Cosham; Petty Officer Stoker Sidney Bevan, aged 29; Electrical Artificer Arthur Edney, aged 34 and from North End; Petty Officer Percy Morgan, 32 and from Tipner; Leading Seaman Harry Wood, aged 28; and Leading Seaman Albert Ford from North End. Arthur Edney had been awarded the Distinguished Service Medal (DSM) on 28 June 1940 for 'daring, endurance and resource in the conduct of hazardous and successful operations in His Majesty's Submarines against the enemy'.[13]

Perhaps the most active submarine with connections to Portsmouth was HMS *Triumph*. A 'T'-class boat, she had been built by Vickers and commissioned on 2 May 1939, only months before the outbreak of war.[14] She displaced 1,090 tons surfaced and was manned by a crew of fifty-nine, with a number of Portsmouth men on board. Electrical Artificer First Class Arthur Biggleston was born in Hayle, Cornwall, on 3 April 1905.[15] Joining the Royal Navy straight from school as a boy seaman at the age of 15, he spent several years on board training ships before joining the Submarine Service later in his career. By the beginning of the Second World War he had settled in Portsmouth, living in Collingwood Road in Southsea.[16] Also on board the *Triumph* was Petty Officer Frank Collison from Lonsdale Avenue in Cosham.[17]

HMS *Triumph*'s war began almost immediately, with patrols of the North Sea, and in December 1939 she was seriously damaged by a mine off Norway – an incident for which she received much publicity[18] – and had to return to Britain for extensive repairs that lasted for six months. After returning to sea she continued patrols off Norway. In late 1940 a decision was made to reinforce the submarine fleet in the Mediterranean by transferring boats from Britain and forming the 14th Submarine Flotilla in Malta.[19] In 1941 the war in North Africa was precariously balanced, with the British army fighting the Italians and Rommel's Afrika Korps in the Western Desert. Axis supply lines ran from Italy across the Mediterranean to Libya, and British submarines were hard pressed attempting to stop these vital supplies from reaching Axis forces.

Arriving in Malta on 14 January 1941,[20] *Triumph*'s service in the Mediterranean was active from the start. In February 1941 she landed commandos for a raid on the Appulian coast. In May 1941 she sank two enemy ships off Calabria, Italy and in the same month sank an Italian auxiliary off Benghazi, Libya. Then in June she had a notable success in sinking the Italian submarine *Salpa* off Mersa Matruh, Egpyt. In July she sank an Italian freighter, and also the gunboat *Dante de Lutti* which was escorting her. After undergoing repairs in Malta, the *Triumph* returned to sea in August 1941, attacking and damaging the Italian cruiser *Bolzano* in the same month.

In January 1942 HMS *Triumph* set off for a patrol from Malta, and was never seen or heard from again. She is believed to have been sunk by a mine in the Aegean Sea on or around 20 January 1942, with the loss of all hands. On board was Electrical Artificer First Class Arthur Biggleston, 36; Petty Officer Frank Collison, 29; and also Engine Room Artificer Fourth Class Herbert Russell, all from Portsmouth.

Tragically, only days before HMS *Triumph* is believed to have been sunk, both Biggleston and Collison were awarded the DSM. Announced in the *London Gazette* on 16 January 1942, their DSMs were for 'courage, skill and resolution in successful submarine patrols'.[21] Both were subsequently awarded a posthumous Bar to their DSM, gazetted on 5 May 1942 for 'daring, enterprise and devotion to duty in successful patrols in HM Submarines'.[22]

Electrical Artificer Arthur
Bigglestone DSM and Bar of HMS
Triumph. (RN Submarine Museum)

The award of a DSM and Bar in such quick succession to both Biggleston and Collison was a rare honour indeed, and a fitting tribute to brave service in extremely difficult and dangerous conditions. Both were older family men who had made Portsmouth their home, and are fine examples of the service shown by Portsmouth's submariners.

Another Portsmouth submariner to be highly decorated was Lieutenant Charles Lambert, who was 24 and from Southsea, and the son of Major General H.P. Lambert CBE, DSC.[23] Joining the Royal Navy as a cadet in May 1937,[24] Lambert served on board the cruiser HMS *Kent*[25] and the minesweeper HMS *Selkirk*,[26] before joining the Submarine Service in September 1940. After joining HMS *Unbeaten*, Lambert was awarded a DSC and Bar for gallant service in the Mediterranean. His first DSC was announced on 3 April 1942 for 'courage, skill and coolness in successful submarine patrols',[27] and the Bar came soon after on 17 July 1942.[28] After taking a submarine command course in late 1942, Charles Lambert took over command of *P615* on 17 October 1942.[29]

P615 had originally been built by Vickers for the Turkish navy, but in 1940 was taken over by Britain. *P615* was serving in West Africa in 1943, providing training for submariners and anti-submarine exercises for surface vessels. On 18 April 1943 *P615* sailed on a patrol. During the night she lost contact with her accompanying minesweeper, and a few minutes after regaining contact the next morning, *P615* blew up and sank within five seconds. She had been torpedoed by the German submarine *U-123*.[30] All hands were lost. Also on board from Portsmouth were Petty Officer Cook Albert Taylor and Petty Officer Clarence Hubbard, aged 33 and from Milton. Albert Taylor had been awarded the DSM in the 1941 New Year Honour list for 'outstanding zeal, patience and cheerfulness'.[31] Charles Lambert himself had been married in April 1941, only a year previously, and had just turned 24.[32]

The last Portsmouth submariner to be lost in action was 39-year-old Petty Officer Stoker Thomas McCauley, on board HMS *Stratagem* on 22 November 1944. The *Stratagem* had been operating out of Ceylon, and is believed to have been depth charged in the Malacca Straits off Malaysia. Only eight men survived to be rescued by the Japanese, of whom only three survived captivity.[33] The fate of the *Stratagem* and her crew only became known when the survivors were liberated from prison camps after Japan surrendered.[34]

Several observations are clear when looking at submariner losses during the Second World War: many submariners were older, experienced sailors, with those from Portsmouth in their late twenties, thirties and a few in their early forties, and most transferred to submarines after serving on board surface vessels. This ensured that they were seasoned and trusted ratings able to perform reliably in very difficult circumstances.

Many submariners were also decorated, no doubt thanks to the active and dangerous nature of their work, and of 113 Portsmouth submariners killed between 1939 and 1945, twenty-five were awarded a total of twenty-nine decorations. It is also noticeable that many leading seamen, petty officers and warrant officers were awarded the DSM – evidence, if any were needed, that the presence of such men paid dividends under the waves.

The Royal Naval Submarine Museum in Gosport pays tribute to their sacrifice, and the museum ship HMS *Alliance* gives a unique experience of what it must have felt like to live and serve on board a submarine in the Second World War.

6

Per Mar Per Terram: The Royal Marines

AS THE HISTORIC home of the Royal Navy, Portsmouth had long been one of the main bases for the Royal Marines. The lineage of the Royal Marines can be traced back to 1664, when the Duke of York and Albany's maritime regiment of foot was formed as an infantry unit to serve at sea on board Royal Navy ships, and the Royal Marines have been a part of the history of Portsmouth ever since. As one of the main manning ports of the Royal Navy, it was logical to establish a Royal Marines base in the city, and the corps was located in several sites in the Portsmouth area before the Eastney barracks were built in 1862. In total, 116 Royal Marines from Portsmouth are known to have been killed during the Second World War. As with sailors, many Royal Marines did not originally come from Portsmouth, but settled there during the course of their careers.

The interwar period found the Royal Marines very much in a state of flux. The Royal Marines had originally been formed from two separate branches, the Royal Marine Artillery and the Royal Marine Light Infantry, which were amalgamated in 1923. In 1924 a government committee had seriously considered disbanding the corps altogether. The Royal Marines survived, however, in a state of limbo, with the Admiralty seeing them as a low priority, and the army questioning their purpose.[1] Sea service was seen very much as the corps' priority in 1939, to support the Royal Navy by providing 'sea-soldiers' and gunners for service on board Royal Navy warships.[2] There was very little development of new forms of warfare, and the debacle at Gallipoli in 1915 had led to a lasting suspicion of amphibious warfare in the Royal Navy[3] and scepticism among most senior Royal Marines.

When war was declared, many marines were still performing sea duty, such as manning guns and providing bands on board the larger warships – nine Royal Marines from Portsmouth were lost when HMS *Royal Oak* was sunk on 14 October 1939. However, the Royal Marines were increasingly forced to carve out new roles for themselves, and also began to take on the commando role, for which they would become famous after the war. Royal Marines personnel also manned landing craft. In order to perform this myriad of tasks, the corps' ranks swelled

A Royal Marine kissing his partner goodbye outside the Royal Marines barracks in Eastney. Sailors and marines could often be away from home for years on end, and separation was commonplace for many Portsmouth families. *(The News 197)*

with a large intake of new men, reaching a total of 78,400 marines of all ranks in 1944. Of this number, 63,000 men were 'hostilities only' – conscripts called up during wartime.[4]

The Royal Marines Band Service continued to provide musicians for the Royal Navy, such as buglers. There were full bands on most of the larger ships, and also at many shore establishments. One manner in which the Royal Marines did attempt to learn from the mistakes of the Great War was in the creation of makeshift harbours, especially after Gallipoli, where men and supplies had to be landed in small boats on open beaches. The Mobile Naval Base Defence Organisation (MNBDO) was formed in 1923 to consolidate captured or makeshift dockyards in active theatres. The organisation was originally based at Fort Cumberland in Eastney, and experimental beach landings were carried out on Eastney beach in the 1920s, leading to the first British landing craft.[5]

A Royal Marine division was in existence at the beginning of the war, echoing the Royal Naval Division of the First World War with battalions of Royal Marine Infantry. It remained inactive, however, as the corps resisted any attempt by the army to absorb it.[6] Eventually the Royal Marines embraced the commando concept, forming nine commando units by June 1944. These fought in north-west Europe, Italy, the Adriatic and in the Far East.[7]

Colour Sergeant Frederick Bird's grave in Highland Road Cemetery, a stone's throw from the Royal Marines barracks at Eastney. *(Author)*

Many of the Royal Marines' early losses in the war were on board ships. Marine William Lambard, 20 and from Southsea, was killed on 13 December 1939 when HMS *Ajax* was hit seven times by the *Graf Spee* during the Battle of the River Plate, killing sixty-one men in total. Three Royal Marine bandsmen from Portsmouth were killed when the aircraft carrier HMS *Glorious* was sunk off Norway on 8 June 1940: Band Corporal John Paumier, aged 27; Musician Albert Jones, 27 and from Eastney; and Musician Reginald Harriman, 20 and from Southsea. Thirteen Marines were lost when HMS *Barham* was sunk in the Mediterranean on 25 November 1941. Among them was Boy Bugler George Miller, aged just 17.

Royal Marines also died at home when not on active service. Sergeant John Maker, aged 25 and from Southsea, died on 25 November 1942 and was buried in Highland Road Cemetery, Southsea. For being the best recruit in his squad during basic training, Sergeant Maker had been awarded the Kings Badge, an award unique to the Royal Marines.

One of the oldest and most experienced Royal Marines from Portsmouth to die during the Second World War is also is buried in Highland Road Cemetery. Colour Sergeant Frederick Bird, 62 and from Southsea, died on 25 October 1943, a remarkable forty-five years after he had first enlisted as a Royal Marine. Several things seem very interesting about Colour Sergeant Bird. Firstly, he was very old to be in the armed forces, even in an administrative or training role. Colour sergeant is the Royal Marines equivalent of an army staff sergeant, and it appears that Bird was based at the Royal Marines barracks at Eastney. But secondly, and most interesting of all, he was a holder of the Russian Cross of St George, Fourth Class. This was a decoration introduced by Tsarist Russia for bravery in action, and was abolished by the Soviets after the Russian Revolution.

Colour Sergeant Bird's service record reveals all.[8] Born on 8 November 1880 in Wandsworth, London, he enlisted in the Royal Marines in 1898, when he was 17. Although he joined the Royal Marines Artillery – at a time when the Royal Marines still consisted of separate branches of artillery and light infantry – he spent most of his service on board ships, probably as part of a gun crew. He was present at the Battle of the Falklands Islands on board HMS *Inflexible* in 1914; in support of the Gallipoli campaign in 1915; and at the Battle of Jutland in 1916, also on board *Inflexible*. It was for his service at Jutland that Bird received the Cross of St George from the Russian Government. Often during wartime, allies will award medals to men from other nations, often on a reciprocal basis, and it seems that Bird was selected to receive a Russian decoration. Sadly, no records survive to explain why Bird in particular received the award. He served in the Royal Marines until 1922, when he was transferred to the Royal Marines Reserve. He carried on in this capacity until 1930, when he turned 50, and was then discharged. When the Second World War began in 1939 and the Royal Marines were desperate for manpower, retired personnel were recalled to serve in supporting roles, freeing up younger men for active service. Bird was recalled as a drill instructor, until he was discharged on 20 October 1942, only five days before he died. That he died so soon after leaving the service suggests that he may have been seriously ill when he was discharged.

With the onset of war the navy's reserve fleet was reactivated, and Royal Marine complements and bands had to be found for these recommissioned ships.[9] Bands were also formed to serve at shore establishments and to tour the country, performing in places such as factories. Music could play a vital role in maintaining morale on a ship, and, in addition, marine bandsmen were trained to operate the ship's gunnery control transmitting station in action.[10] By 1941 there were eighty-four Royal Marine bands, with 1,955 officers and men in the band service, and up to 1,000 bandsmen were afloat at any one time.[11] Each band was led by a bandmaster and assisted by a band corporal, with the number of musicians depending on the size of the ship. The band on HMS *Hood* numbered seventeen, all of whom were lost when she was sunk.[12] The Royal Marines Band Service sustained significant casualties during the Second World War, and twenty-one bandsmen from Portsmouth were lost, mainly when their ships were sunk in action. Three were lost on HMS *Glorious*, HMS *Barham* and on HMS *Hood*. Four bandmasters from Portsmouth were killed during the war: Ronald Chard, 28 and from North End, on board HMS *Barham*; Frank Roe, 33 and from Milton, on board aircraft carrier HMS *Hermes*; Donald Joyce, from Southsea, on board the cruiser HMS *Neptune*; and Albert Erridge, 29, on board HMS *Phoebe*.

The ill-fated Dieppe Raid of 1942 provided one of the first opportunities for the new Royal Marines Commandos to prove themselves in action, and one marine in particular found himself in the thick of the fighting. William Rhodes was born in Ascot in Berkshire on 30 January 1906. He joined the Royal Marines on his seventeenth birthday in London, and underwent his initial training at the Royal Marines Depot in Deal, Kent. Rhodes spent much of his time either in the Eastney barracks in Portsmouth or performing sea duty on board ships, including the battleships *Barham*, *Benbow*, *Emperor of India*, *Ramillies* and *Iron Duke*. Like many Royal Marines, Rhodes seems to have spent more time at sea than many sailors, but married his wife Hilda in Portsmouth in September 1932. When war was declared, Rhodes was on board the battleship HMS *Ramillies*, before spending time on board the cruisers *Orion* and *Liverpool*, and then the aircraft carrier *Illustrious*. When she was out of action after colliding with the aircraft carrier *Indefatigable* in December 1941, Rhodes was discharged to the Royal Marines Chatham Depot.[13]

Although he had spent the majority of his career on board ships, William Rhodes was among the first volunteers for the new Royal Marines commando unit, 40 Commando, which was formed on 14 February 1942. He joined the next day and 40 Commando landed at Dieppe on 19 August 1942, in the second wave. They were originally intended to act as floating reinforcements, but in the event were landed on the open beaches in the centre of the town, suffering grievous casualties, including their commanding officer. A total of 370 men sailed with the commandos, twenty-three of whom were killed, with seventy-six wounded and many more captured.[14]

Despite the failure of the operation, it allegedly provided valuable lessons that were put into place for the invasion of Normandy on D-Day. However, modern historians have suggested that the raid was launched by Lord Louis Mountbatten without formal approval from his seniors, and the story about 'lessons being learnt' was propagated afterwards to cover up the poor planning and execution of the operation, and the heavy losses suffered, particularly by Canadian troops. The raid remains highly controversial to this day, especially in Canada.[15]

Lord Mountbatten, a member of the royal family and a favourite of Winston Churchill, was certainly used to getting his own way and bending the rules. He was also a master of self-promotion, so the story of 'lessons for D-Day' is hardly surprising. In truth, it should not have taken the deaths of almost a thousand men to learn these lessons: it was obvious even before the raid that it would be folly to attempt a frontal attack on a well-defended port. Many of the unique projects that aided D-Day, such as the Mulberry artificial harbours, had already been conceived before Dieppe.

A total of 962 Canadian, British and American men were killed at Dieppe – unbelievably high losses for one day of battle. Among them was Marine William Rhodes, who was killed on 19 August 1942. He is remembered by a special memorial at Pihen-les-Guines Cemetery, France, which suggests that his original grave has been lost. His loss in action with the commandos, after spending so long on sea duty, illustrates just how much and how fast the Royal Marines were evolving.

After returning from Dieppe, 40 Commando was sent to the Mediterranean, where another Portsmouth man died whilst serving with the unit. Lieutenant Norman Longland had been sent out to join 40 Commando in Italy as a replacement for another officer, but became ill and died of hepatitis on 2 March 1944. He is buried in Caserta War Cemetery, Italy.[16]

Several Royal Marines were killed whilst serving with the Mobile Naval Base Defence Organisations. Marine George Butler was killed on 14 September 1942, serving with MNBDO Group I, who had gone to serve in the Far East. He had previously worked for the Portsmouth Electricity Company. Captain Frederick Gleave, aged 47 and from Eastney, was also serving with Group I and was killed on 14 May 1943. Several MNBDO marines were killed in Sicily with MNBDO Group II, including Quartermaster Sergeant Raymond Milbourne, aged 36 and from Southsea, who was killed on 21 December 1943, and Corporal Leslie Denny, aged 24 and also from Southsea, who was killed on 31 December 1943. One historian has written that Sicily saw the most effective use of the MNBDO concept, when the group provided signals, medical, security and malaria control in captured ports in Sicily, and carried out 50 per cent of the unloading of supplies from ships.[17] Towards the end of the war the MNBDO groups were broken up, although Royal Marines landing parties carried on the concept, particularly on D-Day.

The Royal Marines were heavily involved in operations on D-Day, the initial landings seeing the largest ever commitment of Royal Marines in one battle: on board ships, in commando units, crewing landing craft and in landing parties. Royal Marines provided over two-thirds of the landing craft used on D-Day.[18] Sergeant Arthur Bradley, 25 and from Southsea, was serving with 47 Commando when he was killed on D-Day Plus 1, and is buried in Bayeux War Cemetery, France. On the first day 47 Commando had landed with the objective of capturing the small harbour at Port-en-Bessin, where the PLUTO fuel pipeline would later be operated from. He had been Mentioned in Despatches in 1942 for service on board ships during the Malta convoys. His transfer from sea service to the commando role again exemplifies just how much the Royal Marines had changed in a short few years, fighting in ways that might have been unthinkable in 1939.

Several marines from Portsmouth were killed whilst crewing landing craft, particularly in the amphibious operations later in the war. Eighteen-year-old Marine Frederick Derrick was a crew member of HM *Landing Craft Gun (Large)* 15 when she foundered in heavy seas during her maiden voyage on 25 April 1943, and is buried in Milford Haven, Wales. HM *Landing Craft (Flak) 1*, which was a large landing craft bristling with flak defences for the Normandy beachhead, was lost on 17 August 1944. It is believed that she was hit by a manned torpedo. Out of a crew of eighty-six, only two men survived. Among those lost were two Portsmouth marines – Sergeant Frederick Charles, from Cosham, and Marine Alfred Tindall, 33 and from Southsea. They were both lost at sea and are therefore remembered on the Portsmouth Naval Memorial.

The Royal Marines were also involved in a little-known amphibious campaign late in 1944 – the clearing of the Scheldt Estuary in Holland, in order to open up the approaches to the vital port of Antwerp. On 31 October 1944, 48 Commando set sail from Ostend and landed on Walcheren at 9.45 a.m. the next day. After a week of hard fighting, which was made even more difficult by the fact that most of the island is below sea level, the Germans finally surrendered on 9 November. Marine Charles Ware, 29 and from Copnor, was serving with 48 Commando when he was killed on 8 November, the day before the end of the fighting on Walcheren. He is buried in Bergen-op-Zoom War Cemetery, Holland.[19]

Royal Marines were also involved in inland operations near the end of the war. Lance Corporal Edward Ambler, aged 27, was serving with the Royal Marine Engineers in Holland, probably as part of the preparations for the crossing of the Rhine later in March 1945, when he was killed on 2 March 1945. He is buried in Mook War Cemetery, Holland. Royal Marine Engineers are also known to have been active in north-west Europe assisting in building barracks and accommodation camps as the Allies advanced towards Germany.[20]

The Royal Marines ended the Second World War having carved out a significant new role. To this day the Royal Marines Corps have provided Britain with a commando brigade, and have proven to be first-class amphibious units. In recognition of their sterling service in the Second World War and before, the corps was awarded the Freedom of the City of Portsmouth in 1959.

Sadly, the Royal Marines barracks at Eastney was gradually wound down in the post-war years, until the last Royal Marines finally left Portsmouth in 1991, after 240 years of presence in the city. The Royal Marines Museum remains, however, in the former officers' mess, and provides a lasting memorial to the many Portsmouth marines lost in the Second World War and other conflicts.

PART TWO
THE ARMY

7

Pompey's Tigers:
The Hampshire Regiment

THE SECOND WORLD War saw the British army fielding more specialised and diverse units than ever before: artillery, engineers and increased armour, to name but a few. However, the most casualties were still suffered by the foot soldiers, the 'Poor Bloody Infantry'. The Hampshire Regiment was Portsmouth's county infantry regiment. Traditionally, young men joining the army would almost always join their local regiment, especially infantry regiments. Therefore, a large proportion of young men from Portsmouth fought with the Hampshires, both pre-war regulars and wartime conscripts.

The Hampshire Regiment was established in 1881, from the 37th and 67th Regiments of Foot. Prior to 1881 British army infantry regiments were numbered, but widespread reforms linked units with geographical areas. The 67th Regiment in particular could trace its south Hampshire roots back to its formation in 1782.[1] In 1826 the regiment was awarded the nickname of the 'The Tigers' by George IV, after twenty-one years of unbroken service in India.

The British army is unique in that it is effectively formed of a loose band of tribes. The loyalties of most men were, and still are, to their regiment first and foremost, and to the army second. The regiment is the focus for *esprit de corps* and comradeship.[2] These loyalties were further heightened due to many regiments being recruited on a local, mostly county, basis. These loyalties were most strongly felt by men who had joined the army in peacetime and had been 'brought up' in the traditions of their regiment, whereas wartime conscripts tended to think of themselves as soldiers only for the duration of the war and were arguably less bound by loyalties.[3] During the Second World War, the army transferred men from one regiment to another when manpower shortages became acute, and on several occasions men nearly mutinied over the prospect of leaving their 'family'.[4] Regiments develop proud histories and identities over hundreds of years, in contrast to many other countries, where men still serve under a regiment with a number, rather than one with a name.

After the grievous losses suffered during the First World War, in particular by the Pals battalions, recruiting for the infantry became more dispersed. The authorities realised that if

The grave of Private George
Gillard, in St Mary's churchyard,
Portchester. *(Author)*

the majority of the male population from a single community were killed in one battle, the
effect on morale at home could be enormous – something akin to the loss of a battleship.[5]
Current research suggests that between 1914 and 1919, at least 580 Portsmouth men died
serving with the Hampshire Regiment – many of them on single days, particularly on the
first day of the Somme and at Passchendaele. The impact of these huge losses in one fell
swoop was acute. We only need to imagine the devastating effect of hundreds of families being
informed of the loss of loved ones on one morning to understand how heavy casualties could
hit communities very hard.

If, however, men were posted to more diverse units, losses would be spread more thinly. Thus,
during the Second World War many Portsmouth men found themselves serving in unusual
infantry regiments – such as the Black Watch and the Royal Welsh Fusiliers, or even the King's
African Rifles. Although it might be thought that a Portsmouth man would be unhappy about
being in a Welsh or Scottish regiment, research suggests that men, particularly those who were
wartime conscripts, were not overly concerned about what unit they served with, as long as
they were allowed to build and maintain loyalties with the men around them.[6]

Most infantry regiments began the war with two regular battalions and, in addition, several
Territorial battalions. Shortly before the war began the Territorial Army was expanded, and
the Hampshire Regiment eventually sent two Territorial battalions overseas: the 1/4th and

the 2/4th. These two battalions were formed by dividing the pre-war 4th Battalion in two and then expanding each into two new battalions, hence the numbering. In addition, two wartime service battalions fought overseas, the 5th and the 7th. Thus the Hampshire Regiment committed six battalions to active service during the Second World War.[7]

The horrors of the First World War had cast a long shadow over British society, and men, well aware of the sacrifices of their fathers' generation, joined up in a more sober manner than the patriotic enthusiasm seen in 1914. During the early years of the war the British army had to train many thousands of young men quickly, most of whom had no experience of the military at all. Peter Ellis recalled his memories of joining the regiment:

> Well, I suppose the basic training is the way that you get men to operate together. Marching, drilling, arms training, range firing, it all went towards making a unit that was a fighting force.[8]

Although losses did not reach anywhere near the levels of the Great War, 115 men from Portsmouth are known to have died serving with the Hampshire Regiment between 1939 and 1947. The first Hampshire to die was Private Frederick Marchant, 27 and from Wymering. He died on 27 November 1940, and is buried in Kingston Cemetery. The final Hampshire to die was Private Herbert May, aged 36. He was serving with the 2nd Battalion when he died on 24 April 1947, and is also buried in Kingston Cemetery.

The Hampshires were not heavily involved in many of the war's early campaigns, as the 1st Battalion was overseas and the 2nd Battalion was not sent to France until late in the 1940 campaign, which resulted in the evacuation from Dunkirk. The 2nd Battalion suffered few casualties in France, and none from Portsmouth. The 2nd Battalion was also one of very few units to return from Dunkirk relatively unscathed and with most of their weapons.

Many of the regiment's early casualties were members of depot battalions, and probably died of illness at home in England. Many of these early casualties were older men who were unfit for active duty but were serving in a training or administration role. Private Frederick Prince, aged 52 and from Copnor, died on 20 April 1941. He was serving with the 13th (Home Depot) Battalion, and is buried in Christ Church Cemetery, Portsdown. Private George Gillard, 53 and from Copnor, died on 1 October 1941. He is buried in St Mary's churchyard, Portchester. Men who died at home of illness or other natural causes are often overlooked, but they also played a vital role in the war effort by freeing up younger men for active service.

The 1st Battalion, meanwhile, had been overseas for some years, including spells in Turkey, India and Egypt. The battalion began the war in Palestine, but in 1941 found itself based on the besieged island of Malta as part of the 231st 'Malta' Infantry Brigade. Two Portsmouth men died on Malta – Private Lorenzo Beabey, aged 25, who was killed on 29 August 1941 and buried in Pembroke Cemetery, Malta; and Sergeant George Tolcher, 27 and from Cosham, who was killed on 29 November 1941 and buried in Imtarfa Cemetery, also on Malta. Malta played a pivotal role in the Mediterranean war, as a British possession but also perilously close to Italy. For a period during the Second World War Malta became the most bombed place on earth, and for some time the threat of an Axis invasion was very real.[9]

The other battalions of the Hampshire Regiment had been training hard in England for several years, without seeing action or going abroad. With the war turning in the Allies' favour, however, that was soon to change. The 2nd Battalion sailed for North Africa in

Men of the 1st Battalion of the Hampshire Regiment relaxing in Palestine early in the war. From a collection of photographs owned by Private Mark Pook MM. *(Kath Connick)*

November 1942, and took part in the battle for Tunis. Particularly heavy losses were suffered during the Battle of Teboura. The battalion was outnumbered four to one, and after a fierce battle they were forced to withdraw.[10] Among the men from Portsmouth killed were Lance Corporal William Searle, 22 and from Stamshaw; Corporal James Randell, 23 and from North End; Private Sydney Preece, 28 and from Fareham; Private George Chapman, 29 and from Southsea; Private Bernard Chinneck, 26 and from Farlington; Private Sydney Pharoah, 22 and from Landport; and Lance Corporal Dennis Ford, 31 and from Stamshaw. After such heavy losses, which saw the battalion reduced to 194 men, the 2nd Hampshires were taken out of the line to reorganise.

In January 1943 the 128th Infantry Brigade left Britain as part of the 46th Infantry Division. The brigade contained three battalions of the Hampshire Regiment – the 1/4th, 2/4th and 5th – and as a result the brigade became known as the 'Hampshire Brigade'. After going into the front line at the end of January, the brigade bore the brunt of a German counter-attack in Tunisia that began on 26 February. The 5th Battalion defended positions at Sidi Nasr, and the 1/4th and 2/4th battalions fought at Hunt's Gap. After a brief respite the brigade went back into action in Tunisia, before the German forces in North Africa surrendered on 13 May 1943. A total of twenty-three men from Portsmouth had been killed with the Hampshire Regiment in the Tunisian campaign, one of the most overlooked campaigns of the Second World War, and it was very much a 'baptism of fire' for the Hampshires.

Once the threat to Malta had been relieved, the 1st Hampshires and the rest of 231st Brigade eventually took part in the invasion of Sicily, joining the 50th (Northumbrian) Division. The 1st Battalion landed on 10 July, and encountered very light opposition. Private William Jarman, 23 and from Milton, was killed on 10 July 1943, on the second day, and is buried in Syracuse War Cemetery, Sicily. Two more Portsmouth men were killed later in the campaign: on 25 July Private Robert White, aged 26; and on 30 July Corporal Alfred Buckner, 25 and from Cosham. Both are buried in Catania War Cemetery, Sicily. In Sicily the battalion suffered 18 officers killed and 286 men killed and wounded.

The 128th Brigade did not fight in Sicily, but were one of the three main assault brigades for the landings on the Italian mainland at Salerno in September 1943. The 2/4th Battalion had

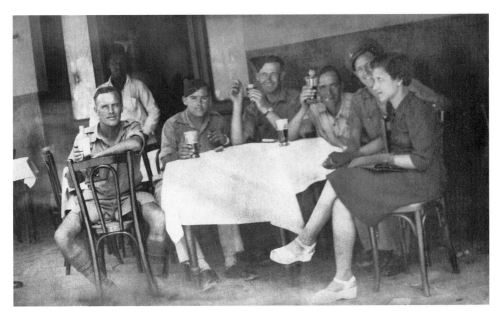

A photograph from the collection of Private Pook showing Hampshires relaxing with a drink in the Middle East. *(Kath Connick)*

left to become a Beach Defence Unit, but the 2nd Battalion had joined in its place. All three battalions in the brigade landed at Salerno on the first day, and met very heavy opposition on the beaches. Three men from Portsmouth were killed with the Hampshire Brigade on 9 September: Private John Hayes, 26 and from Stamshaw; Private Frederick Nimetty, 23 and from Southsea; and Private Edward Smith, 24 and from Copnor.

The 1st Battalion also took part in the landings at Salerno, and one soldier with Portsmouth connections was to distinguish himself in Italy – Private Mark Pook, aged 22 and from East Wittering. Private Pook died of wounds on 9 September 1943 at Salerno, and was awarded a posthumous Military Medal (MM), announced in the *London Gazette* on 11 January 1944.[11] The recommendation for his MM describes his story:

> At Porto San Venere on 8 September 1943, Pte. Pook's Company was counter-attacked by enemy infantry and AFV's [Armoured Fighting Vehicles]. Pte. Pook showed great courage and tenacity in engaging successfully enemy parties with his Bren Gun. He was blown up by a shell burst and temporarily knocked out. On recovering himself he at once got his gun in action again. In this he showed an excellent spirit moving from position to position firing through the grape vines from the hip whenever he could pick out a target. Subsequently, he was wounded in the leg, but continued to fire until exhausted and order by his Platoon commander to withdraw.[12]

The image of a seriously wounded young private, firing his Bren gun from the hip at armoured vehicles through grape vines, is stirring indeed, and it is hard not to think that Pook was unlucky not to receive a higher award. Private Pook is buried in Salerno War Cemetery, Italy.

Another Portsmouth man with the 1st Battalion was also killed on 9 September – Corporal Victor Justice, aged 38.

More casualties were suffered in the Salerno area when the Germans launched counter-attacks against the beachhead. Major Vincent Phillips, 23 and from North End, was a company commander with the 2nd Battalion and was killed on 13 September when the battalion was attempting to move forward; Sergeant William Pinniger, 32 and from Southsea, was killed with the 2/4th Battalion while they were serving on the beaches on 14 September; and Lieutenant William Reed, a 33-year-old intelligence officer with the 5th Battalion, was killed on 16 September on White Cross Hill. The Germans finally began withdrawing from the Salerno area on 20 September. The final man to be killed at Salerno was Private Eric Shepherd, 20 and from Copnor, who was killed on 29 September fighting with the 5th Battalion.

The campaign in Italy has often been overshadowed by D-Day and the liberation of north-west Europe, yet a significant number of Portsmouth casualties – thirty-one men – died in Italy, due to the large number of Hampshire battalions that fought in the Mediterranean theatre. By comparison, twenty-seven Hampshires from Portsmouth died from 6 June 1944 onwards, in France, Belgium, Holland and Germany. Four Hampshire battalions fought in Italy, compared to only two in north-west Europe.

Shortly after the Allies had broken out of the Salerno beachhead, the 1st Battalion was recalled to England, along with the rest of the 50th Division. In total, the battalion had been overseas for a remarkable twenty-three years. Some men had even served with the battalion throughout the entire time they were abroad, with only a few periods of leave at home. It is thought that General Montgomery had specifically asked for the 50th Division to be brought home to take part in Operation Overlord as they had gained significant experience in amphibious operations, in Sicily, mainland Italy and then at Salerno.

Two battalions of Hampshires fought in Normandy, and subsequently through the campaign in north-west Europe. The 1st Battalion, having returned to England from Italy, landed in the first wave on D-Day, suffering four casualties from Portsmouth, one of them receiving a posthumous MM. The 1st and 7th Battalions also suffered significant casualties later in the Battle of Normandy. Peter Ellis' memories of the Battle of Maltot on 10 July 1944 show just how badly the character of a unit could be affected by losses:

> … we attacked Maltot early in the morning and everything went well; too well, in fact, until we had got almost to our position in Maltot village, when the Germans counter attacked and they literally destroyed us. We had no semblance of order left. We lost six guns, six pounders, and we lost almost all our men, killed and wounded. In fact, the 7th Hampshire's were never the same again.[13]

The 7th Battalion lived to fight another day, however. With a chronic shortage of manpower in late 1944, a decision was taken to disband the units of the 50th Division and to disperse the men around other units. Sadly, this included the 1st Hampshires, and the battalion returned to England to become a training unit.

The 7th Battalion fought on, suffering a number of casualties in the stalemate in Holland after Operation Market Garden. Lance Sergeant Harry Oughton, aged 30, was killed on 4 October 1944; Second Lieutenant William Jenkins, 30 and from Southsea, was killed on 5 October 1944;

and Private Elliot Pease, 30 and from Fratton, was killed on 11 October 1944. Oughton, Jenkins and Pease are all buried in Jonkerbos War Cemetery, Holland. Private Arthur Hyde, 29 and from Drayton, was killed on 20 November; and Lance Corporal James Martin, 19 and from Southsea, was killed on 27 November. Both Hyde and Martin are buried in Brunssum War Cemetery, Holland. The 7th Battalion's final casualty from Portsmouth came during the Battle of the Reichswald on 15 February 1945, when Private Edward Searle, aged 21 and from Stamshaw, was killed. He is buried in Reichswald War Cemetery on the Dutch-German border.

Meanwhile, the Hampshire Brigade carried on fighting during the slow and arduous campaign in Italy. One Hampshire battalion – the 2/4th Battalion – was diverted from Italy to Greece to keep the peace during the Greek Civil War, and to prevent communist guerrillas from taking control of the country. The battalion was tasked with clearing the road from Phaleron into Athens and suffered three casualties, one of them from Portsmouth. On 26 December 1944 Lance Corporal Edward Williams, aged 26 and from Sarisbury, was killed. He is buried in Phaleron War Cemetery, Greece. The Regimental History suggests that there was no serious fighting taking place that day, so Williams must have been killed in an isolated incident or died of wounds.

Two battalions of the Hampshire Regiment were later converted to armour and artillery. The 10th Hampshires became the 147th Regiment of the Royal Armoured Corps in November 1941. The regiment landed in Normandy on 2 July 1944, and as part of 34th Tank Brigade was moved around the front depending on which corps or division required tank support. The regiment's first battle took place on 17 July 1944, east of Caen in Normandy. Corporal Charles Mills, 32 and from Southsea, was killed the next day, and is remembered on the Bayeux Memorial, France. The regiment fought on through the campaign in north-west Europe until its last battle in the Reichswald Forest in February 1945. Sergeant Bertram Frampton, 32 and from Southsea, was killed on 15 February, and is buried in Uden, Holland. The regiment was disbanded in October 1945.

In 1938 the 6th Battalion of the Hampshire Regiment had been converted to artillery, becoming the 59th Anti-tank Regiment of the Royal Artillery. The regiment fought with the 43rd (Wessex) Division throughout its existence, with its four batteries being dispersed throughout the division as necessary to provide anti-tank defences. Three men from Portsmouth were killed in action with the 59th Regiment: Sergeant Albert Smith, 27 and from Milton, and Sergeant Louis Hogg, 24 and from Stamshaw, were killed on 10 July 1944; and Bombardier John Nobes, 24 and from North End, died on 1 August 1944.

In 1946 the regiment became the Royal Hampshire Regiment, in recognition of its sterling service during the Second World War, and in 1950 the regiment was awarded the Freedom of the City of Portsmouth. After a succession of post-war mergers, the traditions of the Hampshire Regiment are carried on by the Princess of Wales' Regiment (Queen's and Royal Hampshires), which serves as Portsmouth's local infantry regiment to this day.

8

'Very great powers of command': Major Robert Easton DSO, MBE

ROBERT CORY EASTON was born on 12 June 1915.[1] The son of a Royal Artillery officer, his father had been serving in Gibraltar when he met his Gibraltarian wife, Easton's mother. As a result of his part-Gibraltarian heritage, Easton was remembered by his school colleagues as dark haired and good looking, and with a slightly sallow Mediterranean complexion.

After attending Andover House Prep School, Robert Easton was a pupil at Portsmouth Grammar School from 1923 until 1933. A school prefect, he showed talent for acting and drawing caricatures, and took part in summer cycling holidays, swimming and tennis. He obviously intended to follow a military career, for he was a member of the school's Officer Training Corps during sixth form, and would often gather in the quartermasters store after parades to play in a poker school.[2]

After leaving Portsmouth Grammar School, Robert Easton attended the Royal Military College at Sandhurst on a cadet scholarship. Arriving at the college as a cadet on 1 September 1933, Easton attained the rank of cadet corporal, and in his first term at Sandhurst was awarded a prize for the optional subject of economic history.[3] Public school graduates such as Easton were highly sought after by the armed forces to become officers, as it was felt that they possessed a 'high standard in character'.[4] The Sandhurst of the 1930s focused very much on drill and fitness, at the expense of tactics and strategy.[5]

Easton passed out of Sandhurst in December 1934, and was commissioned soon after as a second lieutenant in the Lancashire Fusiliers on 31 January 1935.[6] He left Sandhurst ranked eighth in his year out of 158 cadets, a creditable performance indeed.[7] While other ranks almost always joined their local regiment, it was not at all unusual for officers to join a regiment to which they had little or no connection. Although Easton left Sandhurst in the top ten of his year, it is telling that he did not join one of the more prestigious guards or cavalry regiments, and instead joined the line infantry. This is probably because prestigious regiments selected their officers based on social connections and wealth rather than ability alone.

Major Robert Easton DSO, MBE. *(Portsmouth Grammar School)*

The British army between the wars had reverted largely to its pre-1914 function – an imperial police force, with many units based overseas, largely in India. Thus the army was relatively small, especially compared to the Royal Navy. Military conservatism had taken root during peacetime, and it was not until the Munich Crisis of 1938 that the British army began to shake off its malaise.[8] Promotion was slow but steady, as many older officers prevented younger men from advancing up the ranks – Easton was not promoted to lieutenant until January 1938.[9] Robert Easton married Patience Faithfull in late 1939. The wedding took place in Bury, the location of the Lancashire Fusiliers Wellington barracks depot, and their marriage may well have been hastened by the onset of war.[10]

When war seemed inevitable in September 1939 the Territorial Army was mobilised, with each infantry regiment having several Territorial battalions. The 1/6th Battalion of the Lancashire Fusiliers initially 'formed up' to begin training at Long Horsley, with Captain Robert Easton as adjutant, and in January 1940 moved south to Newbury in Berkshire.[11] As a Territorial battalion, the men were probably not as well trained as regular soldiers, and so a regular officer like Easton would have a crucial role to play as adjutant – the commanding officer's right-hand man and de facto staff officer.

The battalion left for service in France early in 1940, departing Newbury for Southampton on 14 April. After boarding the troopship SS *Duke of Argyll*, they arrived at Cherbourg the next day. The 42nd Division had been sent to France to reinforce the British Expeditionary Force (BEF),[12] and on 1 May the battalion moved up to the front line at Comines, north of Lille on the Franco-Belgian border. The Battalion War Diary reads very much like those of the First World War – the men were put to work constructing and improving linear defences.

The quiet existence was shattered on 10 May, when Germany invaded Belgium and Holland. Immediately the battalion was ordered to Premesques, and, coming under command of the Line of Communications, the battalion's companies were assigned to guard vulnerable points behind the front line – aerodromes, ammunition dumps and bridges. After several uneventful days behind the lines, on 17 May the battalion was moved to Armentieres, in the front line. From there, the battalion was ordered to move to the area of La Bassee and Carvin, to form a defensive flank for the BEF, as it was feared that an armoured attack was expected in the area of Arras. Already the situation in northern France was becoming desperate, and the battalion was constantly on the move. Interestingly, on 21 May, 'A' Company 'captured' twelve women dressed as nuns, who were – wrongly, as it turned out – suspected of being enemy agents.

Also on 21 May, when the battalion was at Hertain, a report was received that the Germans had broken through the 1st Border Regiment nearby. The 1/6th Lancashires were ordered to counter-attack and restore the situation. 'A' and 'C' Companies advanced without casualties, and the carrier platoon, operating universal carrier vehicles, managed to put one enemy machine gun out of action. The battalion was eventually held up by a railway line, where the enemy were firing machine guns over the embankment, making movement extremely difficult.

The commanding officer went to brigade headquarters, and plans were made for another counter-attack, this time to drive the Germans back over the River Euscat near Proven, and a heavy artillery barrage was arranged to begin at 8.15 p.m. The enemy were driven back across the river, and one platoon of 'B' Company actually crossed the river, but was forced back by the enemy's artillery. The battalion suffered eighty-three casualties, including fifteen men killed, but twenty-three prisoners were taken and the battalion's success was praised by the brigade, divisional and corps headquarters.

After the action at Proven, the battalion gradually pulled back, via Ploegsteert, towards the Channel coast. Eventually organisation all but broke down, and on 29 May the commanding officer took the decision to order a withdrawal to Dunkirk. Retreating to the coast via Rexpoed, the battalion became engulfed in the chaos of the evacuation, and broke down completely. The officers and men were evacuated back to England via the beaches at Bray, and the mole and harbour in Dunkirk.

Robert Easton arrived back in England on 1 June 1940, having been evacuated from the beaches of Dunkirk. For his valuable service in France, Robert Easton was Mentioned in Despatches and made an MBE. The citation for his MBE stated that:

> This young officer of outstanding merit employs unceasingly all his attributes and knowledge to increase the efficiency of the Battalion, which he serves loyally as Adjutant. To all ranks he is an example of discipline, loyalty and self-sacrifice; and he has never spared himself in furthering the interests of the Battalion.[13]

Shortly after returning from Dunkirk, the commanding officer and many of the other senior officers, most of them Territorial, were removed. This might suggest not only how inadequate some of the officers were in action, but also how important Easton had been during the chaotic time in France, as a regular officer and as adjutant and lynchpin of the battalion. This situation was mirrored throughout the army, where it was found that many officers were not as good as they should have been.[14]

During the invasion scare of 1940, the 1/6th Lancashire Fusiliers formed part of the coastal defences of the east coast, first in Yorkshire, and then in Suffolk.[15] Time spent in relatively quiet areas gave a welcome chance to regroup after the evacuation from Dunkirk.

In the summer of 1940 the British army was under pressure to increase its manpower rapidly. As plenty of infantry weapons were available, the easiest way to do this was by forming additional war service infantry battalions.[16] Initially these battalions were crucial for home defence in the event of a German invasion, but in time it became clear that more armoured units would be needed, and the solution found was to convert infantry units to operate tanks, and then transfer them to the Royal Armoured Corps. Subsequently, on 18 July 1941 the 1/6th Lancashire Fusiliers were informed that they would be converted to an armoured unit. Instructors from the Royal Tank Regiment were attached, and armoured warfare courses began almost immediately. Easton himself attended a course in armoured fighting vehicles at Bovington Camp, Dorset, in September 1941. With effect from 1 November 1941, the battalion had fully converted, and became the 109th Regiment of the Royal Armoured Corps.

On 6 November 1941 Robert Easton was promoted to major, after he had handed over his duties as adjutant on 22 October. The coming of war and the rapid expansion of the army had begun to accelerate promotion by merit, enabling gifted young officers to rise through the ranks more easily than during peacetime. On 1 January 1942 he was posted to command C Squadron, and in March 1942 he attended a month-long course at the Royal Armoured Corps Tactical School at Bulford in Wiltshire. Although the battalion had originally been part of the 42nd Armoured Division, in May 1942 they became part of an independent Tank Brigade.[17] In January 1943 Easton was promoted to the substantive rank of captain, while still serving as a temporary major.[18]

The 109th Regiment was not destined to see action as a unit, however. By 1943 it was found that the army had too many armoured units after all, and several of the armoured regiments raised from infantry battalions were disbanded. The men and officers of 109th Regiment were dispersed, and the regiment was formally disbanded on 31 December 1943.[19] While most officers returned to their original infantry regiment, the Royal Armoured Corps obviously had no intention of losing an officer of Easton's calibre, and he was posted to another armoured regiment. The 142nd Regiment of the Royal Armoured Corps had been formed from a battalion of the Suffolk Regiment, in the same manner as the 1/6th Lancashire Fusiliers. They had landed in Algeria as part of the First British Army during Operation Torch, and fought at the Battle of Medjez-el-Bab in Tunisia during the closing stages of the war in North Africa.

Major Robert Easton arrived with the 142nd Regiment on 24 November 1943. Pending another appointment, he acted as second-in-command for a short period while the regiment was resting and refitting at Oued-el-Aneb in Tunisia.[20] The war in North Africa had long finished, but a tough campaign was being fought in Italy, and from early 1944 the regiment prepared to move to Italy.

On 20 April 1944 the 142nd Regiment landed at Naples. They were part of the 25th Tank Brigade, a completely armoured unit that was attached to the 1st Canadian Division, part of the I Canadian Corps. Upon landing in Italy the regiment began intensive training with Canadian units, in particular practising co-operation between tanks and infantry, and also river crossings. Squadrons were detached to co-operate with infantry battalions, in order to give them extra fire support.

The war in Italy had reached something of a stalemate, with the Allies being pinned down on the Gustav Line and making repeated bloody attempts to capture the pivotal point at Monte Cassino since early 1944. An amphibious operation had been landed at Anzio in an attempt to break the deadlock, but had become bogged down. Easton and the 142nd Regiment had arrived just in time to take part in the fourth battle, codenamed Operation Diadem. The intention was to capture Monte Cassino by outflanking it in the Liri Valley, break through the Gustav Line, link up with the beachhead at Anzio and capture Rome.[21]

The operation was launched on 11 May 1944, with the Canadian Corps, including the 142nd Regiment, initially held in reserve to exploit any breakthrough. They did not have to wait long to be called upon. On 16 May, Major Easton's B Squadron was in support of the Royal Canadian Regiment during an attack on high ground at Cardillo, south of Monte Cassino. The terrain was very difficult, consisting of ditches, banks, trees, vines and road embankments. The squadron was very short of ammunition, and was forced to reconstitute itself into a composite troop consisting of only three tanks. A more junior officer might normally have commanded such a small force, but Major Easton took charge personally and supported the Canadian infantry in their attack. The force came under machine gun and sniper fire almost immediately, but Easton kept his headquarters close behind the leading tanks, and his tank was the first to reach the objective. Supporting artillery fire had been promised, but failed to materialise. The Canadian infantry were being heavily mortared, but the tanks remained in position for several hours, with enemy fire increasing all the time. After more tank losses Easton was forced to pull his squadron back, although he remained behind for some time to recover the wounded.

After the battle in the Liri Valley, the Germans fell back on to another defensive position known as the Adolf Hitler Line. On 22 May, Major Easton was in command of a small ad hoc armoured group supporting the 4th Canadian Reconnaissance Regiment in an attempt to outflank the right of the German line near Pontecorvo. The supporting infantry were reported to be less than enthusiastic due to the difficult terrain.[22] Easton commanded his group skilfully, attempting to manoeuvre round the enemy, but they met heavy opposition and three Shermans were destroyed almost simultaneously. Major Easton, in an attempt to get the attack moving, personally carried out a reconnaissance for mines whilst under small arms fire. The force eventually had no choice but to withdraw under the cover of smoke.

The next day, 23 May, the 142nd Regiment was tasked to operate in support of the 48th Highlanders of Canada in an attempt to renew the attack by capturing high ground at Point 106. Both the infantry and tanks were soon pinned down by machine gun and anti-tank fire respectively. Major Easton kept control of his squadron by placing his own personal tank in full view of enemy anti-tank fire, and was in action for twelve hours giving fire support to the Canadian infantry as the force captured the hill. At one point ammunition was so low that the squadron's clerks and cooks were pressed into service carrying ammunition forward, all the time under heavy enemy fire. Just before dark a counter-attack was successfully fended off. The pursuit continued the next day, by which point the regiment had lost so many tanks that they were ordered to reduce the amount of troops in each squadron. One historian called the battle for Point 106 a 'remarkable effort'.[23]

Monte Cassino itself had finally been captured by Polish troops on 18 May 1944 – the fighting in the Liri Valley had outflanked the German defenders and also drawn in their reserves. The Germans fell back from the Gustav Line, and then the Adolf Hitler Line in turn, leaving the way open to link up with the force that had landed at Anzio. On 3 June 1944 the regiment was the first unit of the British Eighth Army to link up with the US Fifth Army at Valmontone. Shortly afterwards, on 5 June, Rome was liberated by US units.

Eyewitnesses reported that throughout the battles in the Liri Valley and on the Adolf Hitler Line, Major Easton showed calmness and a disregard for his own safety, and that his own actions inspired not only his own regiment, but also the infantry fighting alongside them. For his inspired leadership and distinguished service during the May battles, Major Robert Easton was recommended to receive the DSO.[24] The award was announced in the *London Gazette* on 24 August 1944.[25]

Major Robert Easton became the second-in-command of the regiment on 27 July 1944 after the commanding officer had been seriously wounded, leading to the existing second-in-command taking over.[26] This was a slightly different role for Easton, who had been used to being in the thick of the action. The second-in-command frequently commanded the main headquarters to the rear, while the commanding officer was forward with a small tactical headquarters. Easton became far more involved in the battalion's administration – on 22 August, for example, he convened a conference on technical issues connected with Churchill tanks.

The 142nd Regiment fought on in the war in Italy. Later in 1944, Operation Olive, the Eighth Army's attack on the Gothic Line, called for an attack along the Adriatic coast to capture the cities of Pesaro and Rimini. By this time the 142nd Regiment and the rest of the 25th Tank Brigade were part of the British 46th Division, V Corps. The 25th Tank Brigade was initially held in reserve, but V Corps was finding the going difficult in attacking through the hills south-west of Pesaro. On 3 September the brigade took part in an armoured thrust towards the Coriano Ridge and the Marano River, but although the aim was to open the way to Rimini, heavy casualties were suffered and the attack faltered.

It was during this battle that Major Robert Easton was seriously wounded on 2 September 1944. Although the fighting squadrons had moved forwards, regimental headquarters was still in range of enemy fire, and Easton and the intelligence officer were struck by shrapnel at 7.30 p.m. Although he was evacuated to a field hospital, he died of his wounds at midnight the next day, at the age of 29. Tragically, only twelve hours after Easton has been wounded, the regiment had pulled back from the front line for rest. Major Robert Easton is buried in Montecchio War Cemetery, Italy. Easton's obituary in the December 1944 *Portmuthian* remembered him as:

> … being a born soldier … Easton was gifted with considerable talent for drawing in black and white, and possessed of an extraordinarily charming personality.[27]

Robert Easton had served as an adjutant at Dunkirk, and then as a squadron commander and finally a second-in-command in Italy. After being highly decorated and earning such a fine record in action he could have expected to be given the command of a regiment in the not too distant future. He had shown remarkable leadership, flexibility and selflessness under fire, and was Portsmouth's most highly decorated soldier to die in the Second World War.

9

Overlord: D-Day and the Battle of Normandy

PORTSMOUTH HAS BECOME synonymous with the D–Day operation and the subsequent Battle of Normandy. As one of the main embarkation points, and with the Allied Expeditionary Force headquarters nearby at Southwick House, Portsmouth has long been the focus for remembering 6 June 1944, with commemorations every year, particularly on major anniversaries. A significant number of men from Portsmouth lost their lives in Normandy, including twelve men who were killed on D-Day itself.

One Portsmouth man performed especially bravely when serving with the Hampshire Regiment on D-Day. Leslie James Webb, the son of Frederick and Elsie Chalmers, was born in Portsmouth in 1917, the same year that the 1st Battalion of the Hampshire Regiment was fighting at Passchendaele on the Western Front in the First World War. Webb's entry on the Commonwealth War Graves Commission describes him as being from North End, but in 1939 it appears that his family lived at Childe Square in Stamshaw.[1]

The 1st Hampshires were part of the first wave on Gold beach, and were ordered to capture Le Hamel, Asnelles and Arromanches,[2] but the plan went awry almost from the start. After anchoring 7 miles off the coast at 5.30 a.m., rough seas caused serious dislocation to the invasion flotilla. Harry Cripps was serving as a private with the 1st Hampshires on D-Day:

> ... very rough and stormy, and when we landed, we were just thrown on the beaches, and most of the company got drowned, but I was one of the lucky ones who survived, and made the beach head, but got wounded on the beach ... Well, apart from being thrown up on the rough crossing, we were up to our necks in water, and we had so much weight that the ... I was fortunate. I was five foot ten and it came up to my chin. Well, some of the others were smaller, and they never saw ... they just disappeared.[3]

Only two out of the planned sixteen DD[4] swimming tanks arrived on the beach, and aerial bombardment of gun positions at Le Hamel had had little effect. The landing craft 'landed'

The grave of Lance Corporal Leslie Webb MM, in Milton Cemetery. *(Author)*

30 yards from the shoreline, and the men stepped off into 4ft of sea. The Hampshires were pinned down on the beach and could make very little progress. Their commanding officer was twice wounded, and the second-in-command had not arrived.[5]

One of the company commanders took over and devised a plan to get the Hampshires moving and off the beach. 'D' Company was tasked with outflanking Le Hamel and attacking the town from the south-west. Here they found themselves pinned down by a German machine gun position and, as with 'A' and 'C' Companies on the beach, movement became impossible under such heavy fire. Lance Corporal Webb, however, exposed himself to enemy fire in an attempt to get his men moving, braving the heavy fire to get orders from his platoon commander. He was seriously wounded, but his bravery and leadership were a fine example to the rest of the company, who successfully attacked the gun position.

'D' Company ended D-Day in Arromanches. The battalion as a whole suffered 182 casualties of all ranks on D-Day, with five officers killed and eleven wounded. In total, seventy-one of the Hampshires were killed. Four of those killed came from Portsmouth: Private Edgar Loader, 22 and from Buckland; Private David Williams, 29 and from Southsea; Private Charles Gough, 24 and from Copnor; and Private Montague Bishop, 30 and from Portsea. All are buried in Bayeux War Cemetery. Harry Cripps had unpleasant memories of D-Day:

… looking back, my thoughts are with the boys that went over with me, and I know there can't be many left of our company, at least. As I say, I was one of the very, very lucky ones.[6]

Leslie Webb was evidently seriously wounded, and he was evacuated back across the Channel. Sadly, he died of his wounds in the Royal Naval Hospital, Haslar, in Gosport, on 14 June 1944, at the age of 27. The cause of his death was given as 'due to war operations',[7] and he is buried in Milton Cemetery. However, his bravery on D-Day had not gone unnoticed, as almost immediately his commanding officer recommended him for an award. His posthumous MM was announced in the *London Gazette* on 28 September 1944:

At Le Hamel on 6 June 1944, during an attack on an enemy gun position by D Coy, the Company came under heavy enemy fire and found movement forward impossible. L/Cpl Webb, showing complete disregard for his personal safety, repeatedly exposed himself to enemy fire in order to move his men forward. In full view of the enemy he went to get orders from his Pl Comd, and was seriously wounded, but his courage and bravery were such an inspiration to all that the Pl went forward again and seized its objective.[8]

Portsmouth men were also killed on D-Day serving with other units. Lieutenant Michael Burness, 26 and from Southsea, was serving with 4 Commando on D-Day and is buried in Hermanville War Cemetery, France. Staff Sergeant Roy Luff, 23 and from Buckland, was piloting a glider as part of the airborne landings on the east flank of the invasion, and is buried in Ranville War Cemetery, France. Also buried in Ranville are two paratroopers from Portsmouth: Captain George Turnbull, 43 and from Southsea, was the second-in-command of 'B' Company, 12th Battalion, the Parachute Regiment; and Private Ronald Kent, 24 and from Cosham, with the 8th Battalion. Kent is buried in a collective grave, suggesting that he was possibly killed in an air crash.

Private Albert Morrell, aged 22 and from Southsea, was serving with the 2nd Battalion of the East Yorkshire Regiment, and is buried in Hermanville War Cemetery. Sergeant Jack Dunn, 25 and from Balham in London, was serving with 262 Advanced Field Company of the Royal Engineers, and is buried in Bayeux War Cemetery. Private George Kilford, 31 and from Copnor, was serving with 144 Company of the Pioneer Corps, and is also buried in Bayeux War Cemetery.

Although the assault troops on D-Day suffered serious casualties, the losses continued in the days and weeks afterwards as the Allies attempted to consolidate and extend their foothold in Normandy against strong and determined German counter-attacks.[9] On D-Day Plus 1 an unusual casualty occurred. Corporal Roy Henley was a member of 6225 Bomb Disposal Flight, and his landing craft was sunk approaching the beaches. He has no known grave, and is remembered on the Runnymede Memorial to RAF personnel.[10]

Meanwhile, in the Orne bridgehead, the 6th Airborne Division was fighting hard throughout June and July. Private Robert 'Bobby' Johns of the 13th Parachute Battalion was killed on 23 July 1944, and amazingly was found to have been just 16 years of age. He came from a Stamshaw family, and his comrades were astounded to discover his true age after his death. He is buried in Ranville War Cemetery, where his war grave is a poignant sight for many school children of exactly the same age. Bobby Johns is believed to be one of – if not the – youngest British soldier to die in the Second World War.

Private Bobby Johns, who is believed to be the youngest British soldier killed during the Second World War. *(Portsmouth Museums and Records Service)*

Another Portsmouth man distinguished himself serving with the Parachute Regiment in Normandy. Private Sidney Cornell, whose father was African-American, was born on Boxing Day 1914, and appropriately was an amateur boxer before joining up during the war.[11] With a reputation for being 'hard as nails', it's not surprising that he joined the Parachute Regiment. In Normandy, Cornell was a company runner with the 7th Parachute Battalion. On 10 June, 'B' Company led an attack near Le Hom, and despite finding the woods unoccupied, they came under fire from snipers hiding in thick hedges. Not wanting to let the attack become pinned down, the company commander, Major Neal, ignored the snipers and drove the company on until all of the woods had been occupied. He then ordered his men to turn back and deal with the snipers one by one. Major Neal went after one of them himself, along with Private Cornell. The two men worked themselves into a hedge until they got a view of the sniper. Although they managed to kill the sniper, it seems that their target got off a lucky shot, which wounded Major Neal in the leg. Cornell was unhurt.

The 7th Battalion remained at Le Mesnil for some time, but on 10 July 1944 the battalion was ordered to make another raid on what was known as 'Bob's Farm'.[12] The intention of the raid was to secure prisoners of war, who could be a useful source of intelligence under interrogation. The battalion commander Lieutenant Colonel Pine-Coffin again selected

Sergeant Sidney Cornell DCM (middle row, second from left) before D-Day. *(Portsmouth Museums and Records Service 2010/598)*

'B' Company, now commanded by Major Keene, to carry out the operation. The company was severely understrength with only two platoons: one platoon, along with company headquarters, was to occupy the farm, while a second platoon was to clear the surrounding area. Fire support was to be provided by 'C' Company, and also by three batteries of the divisional Royal Artillery. This was evidently an important raid, as the brigade commander, Brigadier Nigel Poett, came forward to 'C' Company's positions to watch the attack. According to Lieutenant Colonel Pine-Coffin, the raid was ordered directly by General Gale in order to assess the strength facing the Airborne Division in the Orne bridgehead.

The preliminary artillery barrage began at 4.35 p.m., and 'B' Company began their attack five minutes later. They immediately came under machine gun fire from the left and heavy mortar fire, and were pinned down in a gully full of landmines. The company targeted the farm with their own small mortars and PIAT anti-tank weapons, with the PIATs[13] in particular producing spectacular results. A small party of the company, made up of one section and company headquarters, including Private Cornell, managed to reach the farm. Pine-Coffin reported that:

> [Major] Keene decided to leave the gully and rush for the farm across the open using [Lieutenant] Pape's Platoon and his own HQ party with the object of getting a foothold in the farm as quickly as possible … Pape's Platoon, together with CSM Prentice, Private Cornell the runner and Private Butler, Major Keene's batman, rushed through the gate and into the farm. All hell was let loose for a few minutes, but soon it was in their hands with some valuable prisoners.[14]

Major Keene was wounded after treading on a mine. The other platoon remained pinned down in the gully, and only one other section managed to reach the farm. By 5.50 p.m., 'B' Company had returned to the battalion's positions, and for some hours afterwards the battalion came under heavy fire. The divisional artillery and the battalion's mortars replied, along with the 13th Battalion's mortars. 'C' Company also replied with a heavy weight of fire, and at one point had to be resupplied with machine gun magazines from the neighbouring 13th Battalion.

The raid caused heavy casualties, with three men killed, Major Keene wounded, along with twenty men, one of whom later died of his wounds. Although the battalion was disappointed, the raid had achieved its objectives in revealing the positions of a number of German machine guns, which forced them to temporarily withdraw from the farm.

Cornell was recommended for a Distinguished Conduct Medal (DCM) after the raid on 18 July, whilst the battalion were still in the line in Normandy. The award was approved, and announced in the *London Gazette* on 1 February 1945:

> This soldier was one of the parachutists who landed behind the German lines in Normandy on the night of the 5th/6th June 1944. During the next five weeks he was in almost continuous action of a most trying and difficult nature. Cornell was a company runner and has repeatedly carried messages through the most heavy and accurate enemy mortar and machine gun fire. Four times wounded in action this soldier has never been evacuated and carries on with his job cheerfully and efficiently. Very many acts of gallantry have been performed by members of the battalion but for sustained courage nothing surpasses Cornell's effort. His courage and many wounds have made him a well-known and admired character throughout not only his own battalion but also the whole brigade. Space does not permit a record of all his feats as he distinguished himself in practically every action and fighting took place daily.[15]

Sidney Cornell's citation concluded: 'He is a truly magnificent parachutist and I cannot recommend him too strongly for a decoration.' It described how he had never failed to deliver a message, even through heavy mortar shelling and well-aimed machine gun fire. The DCM was second only to the Victoria Cross, and was often awarded for 'near misses' for the VC. Cornell's bravery came during a prolonged period of action, including at least three major incidents. If this bravery had been shown in one act, he may well have been recommended for a Victoria Cross. Promoted to sergeant, Sidney Cornell was killed on 7 April 1945, at Neustadt in Germany, when a bridge exploded as he was crossing it.[16] He is buried in Becklingen War Cemetery, Germany.

After the successful landings, Allied forces became bogged down in what some critics perceived to be stalemate, and General Montgomery faced strong criticism for his failure to keep to the targets that he had set prior to D-Day.[17] A number of set-piece operations were launched to attempt to wear down the Germans and then break out of the bridgehead.

The first, Operation Epsom, began on 26 June. Launched out of the Orne bridgehead, Epsom aimed to unleash armoured forces towards the area south of Caen.[18] Sergeant Leslie Scott, 25 and from Eastney, was serving with the 23rd Hussars in the 11th Armoured Division when he was killed on 27 June. He is remembered on the Bayeux Memorial, France. Scott was killed when his Honey tank was attacked by a German tank while he slept. The tank was completely burnt out, and even his identity disks were irretrievable.[19] Captain George Hendry,

A statue of a British soldier during a lull in the Battle of Normandy, outside the D-Day Museum in Southsea. The statue was unveiled in June 1997 by the Duke of Kent. *(Author)*

27 and from Southsea, was killed serving with the 7th Battalion of the Seaforth Highlanders on 29 June. He is buried in St Manvieu War Cemetery, France. The initial objective of Epsom was Hill 112, a feature pivotal to the German defences in Normandy. The 23rd Hussars and 8th Rifle Brigade managed to reach the hill, but were eventually forced to withdraw on 29 June.[20] Although Caen was eventually captured on 9 July, criticism of Montgomery's tactics was mounting.

After Operation Epsom ended, the 43rd Division was given the task of capturing Hill 112, in the little-known Operation Jupiter. The 7th Battalion of the Hampshire Regiment played a key role in the attack, suffered serious casualties taking the village of Maltot on 10 July, and then faced repeated counter-attacks while holding it.[21] The 7th Hampshires lost a total of eighteen officers and 208 men killed, wounded or missing at Maltot. Among them were Private Leslie Daniels, 25 and from Southsea; Private Ronald O'Leary, 26 and from Buckland; Lieutenant Edward Fitzgerald, 21 and from Southsea; and Lance Corporal William Phillips, 39 and from Stamshaw. Daniels and Fitzgerald are buried in Banneville-la-Campagne War Cemetery, France, while O'Leary and Phillips have no known graves and are remembered on the Bayeux Memorial. While the Hampshires eventually had to withdraw, Maltot was finally secured by the division on 15 July.

The D-Day Memorial Stone in Southsea, unveiled by Field Marshal Viscount Montgomery of Alamein in June 1948. *(Author)*

Operation Goodwood was Montgomery's next attempt to break the deadlock in the Battle of Normandy, this time attempting to outflank Caen to the east.[22] Pitting three armoured divisions in an attack out of the Orne bridgehead, Goodwood saw very few casualties from Portsmouth.

Flight Sergeant Kenneth Meehan, 20 and from North End, was a navigator in a Halifax bomber of 158 Squadron, killed when his aircraft was shot down on 18 July during the preliminary aerial bombing during Goodwood. He is buried in Banneville-la-Campagne War Cemetery. Also killed on the same day was Major Clive Modin, 30 and from Southsea. Originally an officer with the King's Regiment, he was serving on attachment with the 2nd Battalion of the East Yorkshire Regiment. He is also buried in Banneville-la-Campagne. Sergeant Harold Thompson, 30 and from Fratton, was killed on 19 July serving with the 2nd Battalion of the Middlesex Regiment, in a machine gun unit attached directly to the 3rd Division. Thompson is buried in Ranville War Cemetery.

The progress of Goodwood was disappointing, and Montgomery called off the operation after only two days. Controversy has raged for years over whether Goodwood really was an attempt to break out or whether, as Montgomery maintained, it was merely launched to wear down the German defenders and tie up their reserves around Caen. Whatever the intention, Eisenhower's frustration at this perceived lack of progress almost cost Montgomery his job.[23]

Unperturbed by the pressure, Montgomery devised another plan for British forces to break out from Normandy, while the Americans were attacking further west. Heavy losses were also experienced in Operation Bluecoat.[24] The 7th Battalion of the Hampshire Regiment was heavily involved in the fighting and suffered considerable casualties. Private Benjamin Broad was killed on 30 July, the first day, and is buried in St Charles de Percy War Cemetery, France. Private William White, 30 and from Eastney, was killed on 2 August 1944 and is buried in Hottot-les-Bagues War Cemetery, France.

On 6 August, the 43rd Division finally captured the crucial Mont Pincon, with the Hampshires performing a crucial role in outflanking and capturing the villages to the north of the hill.[25] Private Stanley Anslow, aged 27, was killed on 6 August 1944, the day that Mont Pincon was captured, and is also buried in Hottot-les-Bagues. Private Percy Hayter, 30 and from Southsea, was killed the next day.

Other Portsmouth men were killed fighting with other units during Bluecoat. Bombardier John Nobes, 24 and from North End, was serving with the 59th Anti-tank Regiment of the Royal Artillery when he was killed on 1 August, and is buried in Bayeux War Cemetery. At the time of Operation Bluecoat, 59th Anti-tank Regiment were directly supporting the 43rd Division. Private Walter Hansford, 19 and also from North End, was killed on the same day, serving with the 1st Battalion of the Worcestershire Regiment, and is buried in Hottot-les-Bagues War Cemetery. Guardsman Henry Batterham, 19 and from Stamshaw, fell fighting with the 6th Battalion of the Welsh Guards on 4 August, and is buried in Bayeux War Cemetery. Private Alfred Teasdale, aged 27, was killed on 6 August with the 4th Battalion of the Wiltshire Regiment, and is remembered on the Bayeux Memorial.

Operation Bluecoat, along with operations by US forces further west, finally broke down the German resistance in Normandy. Despite Montgomery's efforts to conserve manpower, the losses in Normandy had been savage, with many units, in particular the 'Poor Bloody Infantry', suffering casualty rates on a similar scale to those that their forefathers would have known on the Western Front in the Great War.[26]

After Normandy the Allies battled on through France, and after the fall of the Falaise Pocket they quickly liberated Paris, before advancing into Belgium and liberating Brussels. However, many losses were suffered in vicious battles in Holland and Germany before victory in Europe finally came on 8 May 1945. There are many monuments and memorials to D-Day in the Portsmouth area, including the D-Day Museum and Overlord Embroidery in Southsea, fittingly in the home city of so many men who now lie in Normandy.

10

Prisoners of War

THOUSANDS OF BRITISH servicemen were captured in action by the enemy during the Second World War. Although most men captured by the Germans returned safely home, in some cases after years of captivity, sadly a small number died whilst in prisoner-of-war camps. Servicemen captured and held by Nazi Germany faced an arduous experience, many of them for almost five years, but those unfortunate enough to be captured and imprisoned by the Japanese had to endure untold horrors before they were released. It is startling that the death rate for those captured by the Germans was 4 per cent, but for those captured by the Japanese it rose to a horrific 27 per cent.[1]

The bulk of men captured by the Germans entered captivity as a result of the defeats suffered between 1940 and 1942, in Norway, Greece, Crete and North Africa.[2] A particularly large number of British troops were captured in France in 1940 during the withdrawal to Dunkirk and subsequent evacuation.

Some of them seem to have died soon after capture or on the journey to prisoner-of-war camps in the Third Reich. Signalman Alfred Richards, 31 and from Stamshaw, was captured serving with I Corps Royal Signals. He died on 4 June 1940, and is buried in Cadzand, Holland. He must have been taken prisoner and been on his way to captivity in Germany, as British troops did not enter Holland at all in 1940, and that the Dunkirk evacuation ended on 4 June suggests that he had almost certainly been captured earlier in the fighting. Guardsman David Lyons, 32 and from North End, was serving with the 3rd Battalion of the Grenadier Guards. He died on 13 October 1940, long after fighting had ended after Dunkirk, and is buried in Enghien, Belgium. Unfortunately there is little information to suggest why he was in Belgium so long after the fighting had ended.

Once in the prison camps the ordeal was far from over. Sapper Ernest Attfield, 30 and from North End, died on 28 May 1940 and is buried in Sage War Cemetery, Germany. He had been captured serving with 710th General Construction Company of the Royal Engineers. Sapper Kenneth Hill, 21 and from Copnor, was captured serving with 11th Field Company of the Royal Engineers. He died on 29 August 1941, and is buried in Berlin 1939–1945 War Cemetery. Gunner Kenneth Lanyon, 26 and from Southsea, was captured at Dunkirk serving with 194th Battery, 60th Heavy Anti-aircraft Regiment of the Royal Artillery, and died on 30 December 1940. Lance Sergeant John Pearce, 24 and from Southsea, was serving with 5th Battery, 2nd Searchlight Regiment of the Royal Artillery when he was captured, and he died on 21 April 1941. Lanyon and Pearce are both buried in Rackowiki War Cemetery, near Cracow, Poland. Several large prisoner-of-war camps were near Cracow, and graves from these were moved to Cracow after the war.

Although British troops in German captivity were treated relatively well compared to their comrades captured by the Japanese, atrocities were still committed. Sapper Ernest Bailey, 31 and from Paulsgrove, was a member of 9th (Airborne) Field Company of the Royal Engineers. Ernest was the son of Walter and Mary Bailey, and the stepson of Mrs L.E. Bailey. War Office files inform us that Bailey was a very small man, at only 4ft 11¾in tall. He had joined the Royal Engineers in Portsmouth in 1931, and at some point in his life before the war he had broken his nose.[3]

Taking part in Operation Freshman, a daring glider-borne raid on a Norwegian heavy water plant at Vermorsk, Bailey and his comrades were captured by the Germans. Flying in the second of two Horsa gliders, they crash-landed near Lensmannsgard. Several of the group were seriously injured, and therefore the men asked local Norwegians to inform the Germans that they were willing to surrender. They were captured and taken to a prison camp at Slettebø, where they were executed by firing squad between 19 and 20 November 1942. These killings were in accordance with Hitler's 'Commando Order', which had decreed that all captured enemy commando troops were to be executed as spies. Eyewitnesses recorded that the airborne engineers were wearing a mixture of army uniform and civilian clothing, but they were obviously legitimate British soldiers and not spies. Evidence suggests that the men were tortured prior to their execution – most had broken limbs and been struck over the head. Their partially clothed bodies were dumped, without ceremony, in a mass grave on a beach.[4]

After the war, British authorities investigated the shooting of Bailey and his comrades. The firing party themselves were absolved of any blame as they had little option but to follow orders, but Lieutenant General Von Behrens, the local German commandant, and his Chief of Staff, Colonel Probst, were indicted for war crimes.[5] Probst died of cancer shortly before he could stand trial, but Von Behrens appeared before a British Military Court in May 1946. He was found not guilty of ordering the killings, with the members of the court taking only twenty minutes to reach their verdict. Evidence presented to the court suggested that the German army and the Gestapo had argued over whether to kill the men, and that the matter had even been referred to Hitler himself.[6]

With the acquittal of Von Behrens, nobody was ever held responsible for the brutal killings. Sapper William Bailey is buried in Stavanger (Eiganes) churchyard, Norway. A memorial stands at Slettebø, where Bailey and his comrades were executed.

Sadly, prisoners died even after the end of the war in Europe. Private William Starling, 29 and from Milton, was a member of the Royal Army Ordnance Corps, and was attached to the Royal Engineers when he was captured and taken prisoner. It is believed that he was captured early in the war during the series of defeats that began with Dunkirk, as in early 1942 he was being held in Stalag VIIA.

Prisoner-of-war records tell us that Private Starling was later held at Stalag 344, one of the largest camps holding British prisoners, in Lamsdorf in southern Poland.[7] Lamsdorf was known as a rough camp, with an almost 'wild west' reputation.[8] It appears that he had been marched from Lamsdorf during a series of brutal death marches, along with thousands of other prisoners who were force-marched across Germany and occupied Europe in the depths of a terrible winter.[9] Tragically, Starling died only a matter of days after being liberated, his family believe as a result of food poisoning.[10] He is buried in Prague War Cemetery, Czech Republic.

William Starling sent several letters home while he was held captive, which not only give us a valuable insight into life as a prisoner of war, but also how friends and family back home could keep in touch with their loved ones. Starling corresponded with his friend Norman Martin throughout his time in captivity, discussing such things as cigarettes, gramophone records and Portsmouth Football Club winning 16-1.[11] When he wrote to Mr Martin in September 1944 Starling was looking forward to freedom:

> I hope you have bags of gramophone records as I think I may soon be enjoying a convivial get together ...[12]

The Japanese Government had not signed or recognised any of the international treaties on the treatment of prisoners of war, such as the Geneva Convention. As such, the Japanese authorities felt under no obligation to treat prisoners humanely. In addition, Japanese military culture saw surrender as a shameful act, and it was widely felt that people who had allowed themselves to be captured were not deserving of respectful treatment. The 132,142 Allied prisoners held by the Japanese were allowed no access to Red Cross representation and camps were not inspected by neutral countries.[13] Prisoners faced brutal treatment, torture, summary punishment, forced labour, medical experiments, starvation rations and little or no medical treatment. Unsurprisingly, many Japanese personnel were tried and executed for war crimes after the war, and the pictures that emerged of the emaciated men liberated in the Far East shocked the world.

Almost 50,000 British servicemen were captured at Singapore, but their fight for survival was only just beginning. The Japanese kept prisoners of war in barbaric conditions, and many were used for slave labour. Most of the men captured in Singapore in 1942 were initially held in barracks at Changi, outside the city centre – 50,000 men were crammed into buildings designed for a tenth of that number.[14] Later in the war, most of the men were used for slave labour in the Japanese-occupied territories, including on the infamous Burma Railway.

Some men seem to have been kept in Singapore for years, and some died there. Lieutenant Cecil Edwards, aged 41 and from Southsea, died on 24 September 1943; Gunner Stanley Bannier, aged 31 and of Southsea; Gunner Eric Donachie, 25 and from Southsea; and Corporal John Karmy, 23 and from Southsea, all died in Singapore in September 1944. We cannot even begin to imagine the kind of suffering and brutality that these brave young men endured in their years of captivity.[15]

Hong Kong was the main base port of the Royal Navy's China Station, and was attacked by the Japanese on 8 December 1941, eight hours after the raid on Pearl Harbor. Hong Kong eventually fell on Christmas Day 1941, and like Singapore, thousands of men went into a harrowing captivity, from which few would return. Many men who surrendered at Hong Kong

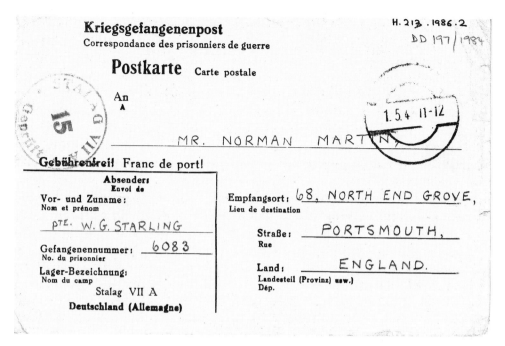

A postcard sent by Private William Starling to a friend whilst he was a prisoner of war in Germany.
(Portsmouth Museums and Records Service)

were lost when the Japanese merchant vessel *Lisbon Maru* was torpedoed and sank whilst sailing between Hong Kong and Japan. Lost on the *Lisbon Maru* were Corporal Walter Hodge, 43, serving with the Royal Signals; Lance Corporal Henry Moxham, 28 and from Southsea, and Staff Sergeant Edward Kehoe, both of 40th Fortress Company Royal Engineers; Lance Sergeant Thomas Newman, 25 and from Cosham, who was serving with 22nd Fortress Company Royal Engineers; and Gunner Arthur Johnson, 26 and from Copnor, of 12th Coast Regiment Royal Artillery. They are all remembered on the Sai Wan Memorial, Hong Kong. Ships taking Allied prisoners to Japan, such as the *Lisbon Maru*, became known as 'hellships'. Out of the 50,000 men shipped to Japan, 10,800 were lost at sea during the journey.[16]

One Portsmouth officer, Captain Robert Bonney, 47 and from Southsea, was murdered by the Japanese after being captured. Bonney had originally served in the ranks for ten years, including during the First World War. Commissioned into the Royal Army Ordnance Corps in April 1938, Bonney and several of his men were captured during the fighting at Repulse Bay. They were killed on 20 December 1941, and are remembered on the Sai Wan Memorial. Also captured in the fall of Hong Kong were many members of the Hong Kong Dockyard Defence Corps. As Portsmouth was a naval dockyard city, many dockyard workers were posted to work in the Royal Naval Dockyard in Hong Kong, and many were formed into a defence corps.

Sergeant Bertie Welsh, 33 and from Buckland, was serving with 22nd Fortress Company of the Royal Engineers when he was captured in Hong Kong, and died on 28 November 1942. Naval ratings were also captured in the Far East. Petty Officer Thomas Watts, 46 and from Cosham, was serving at HMS *Tamar*, the naval base in Hong Kong, and died on

30 November 1942. Armament Sergeant Major Alan Read, 37 and from North End, died on 12 February 1943. He had been serving with the Royal Electrical and Mechanical Engineers when he was captured in the fall of Hong Kong. Private David Blake, 28 and from Copnor, was with the Hong Kong Dockyard Defence Corps, and died on 28 December 1943. Lance Sergeant Harold Kennard, 34 and from Stamshaw, was a member of the Royal Signals, and died on 28 December 1942. He was captured in the fall of Hong Kong and taken to Japan to work as a slave labourer. Private George Ogle, 46 and from North End, was a member of the Hong Kong Dockyard Defence Corps, and died on 5 February 1945. He had also been taken to Japan as a slave labourer, serving over three years as a prisoner of the Japanese by the time of his death.

Due to the long supply lines up to the front line in Burma, the Japanese decided to construct a railway, running from Thailand to Rangoon. Due to the urgency required – they aimed to start work in September 1942 and finish by the end of 1943 – the Japanese used the thousands of prisoners in their custody as forced labour. It is estimated that some 330,000 men – British, Commonwealth, Allied and natives – worked on the Burma Railway, also known as the Death Railway, and 12,399 died, including 6,318 British men. In some groups the death rate reached 50 per cent.[17]

Armament Staff Sergeant Edward Rex, 25 and from Southsea, was serving with the Royal Electrical and Mechanical Engineers when he was captured in Singapore, and died on 5 September 1943. Private Sidney Rich, 31 and from Southsea, was also captured at Singapore with the 5th Battalion of the Suffolk Regiment, and died on 27 October 1943. Both are buried in Thanbuyayzat War Cemetery, Burma.

Many more worked on the Thailand end of the line, all of them having been captured in the fall of Singapore in February 1942. Most of them are buried at Kanchanaburi War Cemetery, Thailand. Gunner Arthur Denmead, 22 and from Fratton, was serving with 135th Field Regiment of the Royal Artillery, and died in June 1943.[18] Sergeant Frank Hudson, 28 and from Landport, was captured while serving with 125th Anti-tank Regiment, Royal Artillery, and died on 5 August 1943. Signalman John Morey, 36 and from Southsea, was a member of 9th Indian Division, Royal Signals, and died on 17 September 1943. Gunner Walter Cottrell, from Southsea and at the young age of 19, was serving with 3rd Heavy Anti-aircraft Regiment, Royal Artillery, and died on 22 October 1943. Lance Corporal Derek Foster, from Southsea and serving with 18th Divisional Provost Company, was 29 when he died on 27 November 1943. Private John Moore was a qualified electrical engineer, who was evidently working in Malaya before the war, and having joined the local volunteer defence force was captured in the fall of Singapore. He was 38 when he died on 19 December 1943. Gunner James Hammond, age 38 and from Fratton, had been captured with 11th Battery, 3rd Heavy Anti-aircraft Regiment, Royal Artillery, and died on 11 January 1944.

At the end of the railway nearest Burma, several Portsmouth men are also buried at Chungkai War Cemetery, Thailand. Lance Sergeant Phillip Lansley, age 31 and from Paulsgrove, was serving with 1st Heavy Anti-aircraft Regiment, Royal Artillery, and died on 9 January 1944. But perhaps the saddest story is that of Captain Cecil Lambert, 60 and from Cosham, serving with the Royal Army Ordnance Corps. He died on 24 June 1943, showing clearly that even the old were not excused from the brutality. That they died in such a terrible manner and so far away from home should never be forgotten.

Many prisoners of war in the Far East were transported to Japan to work as slave labour in mines, factories and shipyards, in particular during the later part of the war when the Japanese were desperate for manpower. Eleven Portsmouth men died and were buried in Japan during the Second World War. Sadly, it is difficult to find out much more about them and their experiences, as neither the Red Cross nor the British Government were able to keep records of them. Both Lance Sergeant Kennard and Private George Ogle are buried in Yokohama War Cemetery, Japan. Many men who had worked on the Burma Railway and were subsequently sent to Japan thought that conditions there were even worse.[19]

Neither should we forget the men who were 'fortunate' enough to survive captivity, whoever their captors. A soldier captured at Dunkirk, for instance, would have spent five years as a prisoner before being liberated in 1945. The lives of many men and their families were deeply affected by their experiences as prisoners of war.

11

Forgotten Army: War in the Far East

ALTHOUGH THE WAR in Europe began in September 1939, for some years there had been mounting suspicions about Imperial Japan's ambitions in the Far East. The Axis alliance between Germany, Italy and Japan only heightened these fears. Britain had particular cause for concern, with important colonies in the Far East, especially in India, Ceylon, Burma, Malaya, Singapore, Hong Kong and Australia. Many of these places would have been familiar to generations of Portsmouth sailors and soldiers, as garrisons and naval bases.

A total of 168 Portsmouth men are known to have been killed in action or died of wounds or illness whilst fighting during the Second World War in the Far East: in Bangladesh, Burma, Ceylon, Hong Kong, India, Indonesia, Japan, Malaysia, Singapore and Thailand. Sadly, their sacrifice has often been overshadowed by the war in Europe – the British Fourteenth Army in Burma in particular has become known to history as 'the Forgotten Army'.

The war in the Far East began on 7 December 1941 with the Japanese navy's surprise attack on the American fleet at Pearl Harbor. Almost simultaneously, the Japanese launched a wave of attacks throughout south-east Asia. For almost the next four years British and Allied troops would be fighting a determined enemy in extremely trying circumstances, and suffering a heavy toll indeed.

Singapore, described as 'the Gibraltar of the East', had been identified as a crucial point in the British Empire that was vulnerable to Japanese attack as early as the 1930s. Singapore was home to an important and state-of-the-art dockyard, which not only supported the Royal Navy's Far East fleet, but also commanded the Straits of Malacca and the sea routes from the Pacific to the Indian Ocean. As such, it became a central point of British foreign policy, known as 'Fortress Singapore'.[1] However, in the style of France's Maginot Line, the only defences built were some formidable gun emplacements facing out to sea, designed to protect the dockyard only. It was thought impossible that the Japanese would come overland through the dense Malayan jungle, and that the guns of the Royal Navy would be able to protect Singapore from the sea.

However, come overland they did; the Japanese landed further up the Malay Peninsula on 8 December 1941, almost simultaneously with their attack on Pearl Harbor. Although their 30,000 troops were easily outnumbered by the 50,000 British and Commonwealth defenders, the Japanese troops took well to fighting in the jungle environment, and could call on strong air and naval support. The few British aircraft in Singapore were obsolete and the Royal Navy found itself understrength in the Far East, particularly after HMS *Prince of Wales* and HMS *Repulse* had been sunk by air attack off the coast of Singapore on 10 December.

Given the loss of sea and air superiority and the lack of reinforcements, it is generally thought that the British commander, Lieutenant General Arthur Percival, could not have done much better. By 15 February 1942 the Japanese had broken through the last line of defence and the British forces were running out of food and ammunition. Percival opted to surrender, and over 130,000 men were captured at Singapore, including 38,496 British troops.[2] The fall of Singapore was the largest ever surrender of British and Commonwealth troops, and the most humiliating defeat that the British armed forces have ever suffered. The myth of Japanese invincibility had been born.[3]

Some 2,000 men were killed in the fighting; many of them garrison troops from the Royal Artillery and Royal Engineers. From Portsmouth, Gunner Gordon Drew, aged 20 and from Cosham, was serving with the Royal Artillery; Sergeant Ernest Bacon, 30, and Sergeant Victor Cole, 27 and from Milton, were killed serving with the Royal Army Ordnance Corps; Private Henry Aldridge, 36 and from Landport, was a member of the Royal Army Medical Corps; Private Frank Cockles, 31 and from Southsea, was serving with the Royal Army Service Corps; and Lance Corporal Harold Bravington, 23 and from Southsea, was fighting with the Royal Engineers. They all have no known graves, and are remembered on the Singapore Memorial. Two RAF personnel from Portsmouth were also killed: Aircraftsman First Class Harold Knight and Leading Aircraftsman Frederick Smith.

Although the fall of Singapore has become one of the most ignominious incidents in British military history, a similar campaign also took place around the same time in Hong Kong. Hong Kong was also an important naval base and the home of the Royal Navy's China Station in peacetime. The garrison in Hong Kong consisted largely of service units and Royal Artillery. The first Portsmouth losses came on 8 December 1941, when Staff Sergeant Lawrence Benford, a 29-year-old from Buckland, and Staff Sergeant Walter French, 35 and from North End, were killed serving with the 12th Hong Kong Company of the Royal Army Service Corps. They are both remembered on the Sai Wan Memorial. On 19 December Lieutenant Colonel John Yale, 44 and from Southsea, was killed. He was a senior officer with the Hong Kong and Singapore Artillery, and is buried in Sai Wan War Cemetery. Also killed on 19 December was Corporal Kerry Ryan, 25, serving with the Royal Army Ordnance Corps, and he is also buried in Sai Wan. Lieutenant Frederick Southwell, 37, of the Royal Signals was killed on 23 December 1941, and is buried in a collective grave in Stanley War Cemetery, Hong Kong.

The wave of Japanese conquests swept on throughout the Far East. In some quarters the myth of Japanese invincibility spread, leading to fears about a collapse of morale amongst British and Allied forces. After landing in Malaya the Japanese invaded Burma, a British colony on the border of India, on 15 December 1941.[4] British troops retreated north during early 1942 and eventually the Japanese managed to push the British forces right back to the India–Burma border. There the line had to be held at all costs to prevent the loss of India, the jewel in the crown of the British Empire. The desperate situation in Burma inspired some innovative thinking from some officers. The Chindit operations were the brainchild of Brigadier Orde Wingate, who had already tested forms of long-range penetration warfare in East Africa. In Burma, he was given the 77th Indian Brigade to train as a force to fight far behind the Japanese lines. They were trained to be supplied with stores dropped by parachute and to use a minimum of heavy equipment. The force was structured into a number of columns, instead of the usual companies and battalions.

Wingate's first plan, Operation Longcloth, was originally intended to have been part of a wider campaign in Burma, but despite the wider offensive being cancelled, Wingate was persuaded to take his men into the jungle anyway. The aim of the operation was to harass the Japanese across the River Chindwin, and also to trial Wingate's concept of long penetration.[5] Beginning their march into Burma on 8 February 1943, they crossed the Chindwin on 13 February.

Lance Corporal George Sullivan, 23 and from Cosham, was serving with the 13th Battalion of the King's Regiment, a unit normally recruited from the Liverpool area, and the battalion played a major part in the first Chindit operation in Burma. Lance Corporal Sullivan was part of a patrol of eight men commanded by Lieutenant Stuart-Jones that set out from 8 Column, then near Pinlibu, to locate brigade headquarters on 6 March 1943. The patrol reported to Brigadier Wingate four days later, completely out of food and near to collapse.[6] At this point Sullivan was ordered to join 142 Commando Company, a special unit under the command of Lieutenant Sprague, and attached to 8 Column, commanded by Major Scott.[7] The 142 Commando had been trained as 'fighting saboteurs' by the famous 'Mad Mike' Calvert, who would later go on to serve with the SAS.[8]

The Chindits stayed in the jungle until late March before Wingate decided to withdraw. They had been fighting the Japanese continually and had often had to leave their wounded behind. Much of their time was spent clearing paths through the dense jungle with kukris and machetes, and of the 3,000 men who set off on the first Chindit expedition, 818 died. Those that returned had covered a total of between 1,000 and 1,500 miles, but only 600 were fit for further military service and it took many months for some of the survivors to return to British lines.

Following an action on the Irrawaddy River on 10 April 1943, Lieutenant Stuart-Jones was ordered to take a patrol out to locate a party of men who had become lost in the jungle. Stuart-Jones picked Sullivan as the only Englishman in his patrol, the rest being Gurkhas. The lost party were soon located, but one of their sections was itself out on a patrol to locate the main body. As the only English-speaking soldier, Sullivan was left behind to guide the missing party back while the rest of the patrol returned east. Neither Sullivan nor the missing party were ever seen again.[9]

It seems that Sullivan was captured by the Japanese some time after 10 April 1943, whilst he was alone in the jungle, although the exact circumstances of his capture are unclear. We do know that he was held in block six of Rangoon Jail, where he contracted beriberi and as a result suffered from dystrophy, a muscle-wasting illness. The hospital at the jail was very poor, with no medical officer for a long time, and sick men were simply laid out to die.[10] Sullivan died at 8.15 p.m. on 2 August 1943, and was buried in Rangoon War Cemetery near the jail.[11] Perversely, while the Japanese captors treated prisoners extremely harshly when they were alive, men who died in captivity were afforded the utmost respect in death. It was only in 1945, almost two years after he had gone missing, that it was confirmed that Sullivan had been lost in the jungle, and only after the liberation of Rangoon was his grave discovered.

Lance Corporal Sullivan was part of one of the most legendary British units of the Second World War, and had taken part in a significant feat of arms. Despite the huge losses, the principle of deep penetration warfare in the jungle had been proven and a much larger expedition was approved for 1944.

Several Portsmouth soldiers were killed in the pivotal battles around Imphal and Kohima on the Indian-Burmese border, as the Japanese launched their last major offensive during 1944. Corporal Harry Lewis, 24 and from Wymering, was serving with 864th Mechanical Equipment Company of the Royal Engineers when he died on 7 April 1944, and is buried at Imphal. Private William Goldring, 20, was with the 1st Battalion of the Berkshire Regiment when he was killed on 23 April 1944, and is buried at Kohima. Gunner Frederick Webb, 24 and from North End, was killed on 28 May 1944 serving with the 82nd Anti-aircraft and Anti-tank Regiment of the Royal Artillery, and is buried at Imphal. Webb's service number suggests that he had originally enlisted in the Hampshire Regiment.[12] Private Henry Lovell, 31 and from Copnor, was serving with the 4th Battalion of the Royal West Kent Regiment. He was killed on 2 November 1944, and is buried at Imphal. The war in Burma eventually turned in the Allies' favour, with the capital Rangoon and much of the country being liberated in 1945.

One Portsmouth officer was decorated for his actions in Burma towards the end of the war: Captain Maurice Budd, from Copnor and an officer of the Royal Sussex Regiment, was serving on attachment with V Force in Burma in 1945. V Force was an intelligence-gathering unit established by the British army in Burma, and was originally formed in 1942 to act as a 'stay-behind' guerilla force. As the war drew on and the Allies went on the offensive in Burma, V Force began to act more aggressively to gather intelligence and set up ambushes.[13] This was often done in partnership with local tribesmen sympathetic to the Allied cause.

Captain Budd was serving with C Group of V Force on 17 January 1945, and was ordered to enter the jungle and establish an intelligence screen around the Arakan, to pass back information to higher headquarters. This was in anticipation of an advance south by Fourteenth Army, and so Budd and his comrades were the advance guard of the liberation of Burma. Budd seems to have served with No 3 Unit of C Group, who initially supported the 26th Indian Division on Ramree Island, before moving into the Taungup area. Their task was then to 'recce' islands along the Burmese coast. Each sub-unit had two officers, with Captain Budd acting as commander of No 3. They were far in advance of the rest of the British forces in Burma and a long way from help. Officers routinely took part in patrols, but also had an important role in analysing and forwarding on intelligence.

The citation for Budd's Military Cross (MC) picks up the story:

During the period under review [16 February to 15 May 1945] Capt. M.A.J. Budd operating continuously with clandestine small patrols behind in the RAMREE & TAUNGUP – SANDOWAY areas has provided a constant flow of valuable information regarding enemy concentrations and movement. On one occasion knowing that the enemy were aware of his presence behind their lines and were hunting him, he remained and completed his task and then succeeded in withdrawing his patrol without loss. Throughout Capt. Budd has performed his duties with unfaltering steadfastness and without personal regard, displaying a standard of courage and devotion to duty of a high order. I strongly recommend him for the award of the Military Cross. [14]

The award was announced in the *London Gazette* on 17 January 1946. [15] However, Budd, who was later promoted to major, did not live to receive his Military Cross. He died on 23 November 1945 at the age of 28, and is buried in Gauhati, India. Budd and his colleagues were, to an extent, the forerunners of the post-war SAS operations in the jungle of Malaya and Borneo.

Although the war in the Far East had been arduous and against a determined enemy, it was largely eclipsed by the fighting in Europe. Therefore it is surely all the more important that we remember the many men from Portsmouth who fought and died so far from home.

PART THREE
THE ROYAL AIR FORCE

12

'Bucky': Wing Commander John Buchanan DSO, DFC

HIS PHOTOS MIGHT show an unwarlike, tall and wiry character, but for offensive spirit, reputation and sheer application, Wing Commander John 'Bucky' Buchanan must have had few equals. He also became one of Portsmouth's most highly decorated servicemen of the Second World War. John Kenneth Buchanan was born on 19 March 1919, the only son of William Archibald Buchanan and his wife.[1] His father had served in the army as a corporal but later became an accountant, based in Elm Grove in Southsea. The Buchanan family originally lived in Kings Road, before moving to Lorne Road in Southsea.

After attending Fairlight Prep School, Buchanan attended Portsmouth Grammar School between 1927 and 1935. Little is known about his time at the grammar school, but Buchanan was a member of the Officer Training Corps, receiving an 'A' grade in the OTC exam in March 1935. He also excelled at the 100-yard run on sports day. Shortly after leaving Portsmouth Grammar School Buchanan undertook flying lessons, first going solo in December 1935 before gaining his 'A' licence on 4 January 1936 in a Gypsy Moth biplane at Portsmouth Airport.[2]

Soon after gaining his pilot licence Buchanan joined the Royal Air Force, and was commissioned in May 1937. Interestingly, Buchanan seems to have not planned for a long career in the RAF, as he was only given a short service commission.[3]

By September 1937 he was an acting pilot officer at 3 Training School, Spitalsgate near Grantham. After completing his initial RAF training, Buchanan was posted to 101 Squadron, who were based at Bicester.[4] Initially equipped with Boulton-Paul Overstrands, an obsolete twin-engine biplane, the squadron re-equipped with Blenheims as part of the RAF's hurried modernisation for war in 1938. The outbreak of war found Buchanan as a flight lieutenant, flying Wellington bombers with 37 Squadron.

Buchanan was awarded the Distinguished Flying Cross (DFC) in 1940 'for gallantry and devotion to duty in the execution of air operations', which are believed to have been over Germany during late 1939 and early 1940.[5] He was also awarded a Belgian *Croix de Guerre*.[6]

Wing Commander John Buchanan
DSO, DFC. *(Portsmouth Grammar
School)*

Later in 1940 Buchanan was posted to the Sudan, where 14 Squadron were converting
to Blenheims. He first appeared in squadron records on 30 October 1940, and subsequently
saw action with the squadron over Eritrea, bombing warehouses, coastal islands, motor works,
railways, naval workshops and enemy positions. He also conducted reconnaissance flights and
anti-submarine patrols.[7]

After their last operation in Sudan on 3 April 1941, Buchanan and the rest of 14 Squadron
moved to Egypt. From there they went to the Western Desert, arriving at Landing Ground 21,
an improvised desert airfield, on 1 May 1941. During their first month in the desert the
squadron suffered horrendous losses in action, including on one occasion losing ten aircraft
and crews in one week. Buchanan, however, must have been in his element, bombing enemy
troop positions and airfields, and for operations in Egypt during 1941 he was Mentioned
in Despatches.[8]

In July 1941, 14 Squadron left North Africa for the relative calm of Palestine. A month later
they moved to RAF Habbaniya in Iraq, shortly after British forces had put down a pro-German
coup. From there they carried out a number of missions dropping leaflets on Iran. Their stay in
Iraq was short, however, for in October the squadron was ordered to return to Egypt. Around
the same time Buchanan was promoted to wing commander and became commanding officer,
a role he retained until May 1942. He was only 22 when he took over command, a remarkable

but not unheard of age for an officer to lead a squadron. In November 1941 they were once again in the Western Desert to support Operation Crusader, targeting Axis enemy troops and tanks in support of the Eighth Army.

While in the Western Desert Buchanan showed an unconventional approach to leadership. According to the 14 Squadron Association newsletter, when the squadron's aerodrome was being repeatedly pestered at 8 p.m. every night by enemy aircraft, Buchanan decided that this was 'a bit much' and contacted a fighter squadron, who promptly arrived at 8 p.m. and shot down the offending Junkers 88s![9] Once again Buchanan took on a very active role in the desert, flying many operations himself. His disdain for paperwork was shown by the fact that he rarely signed the Operations Record Book personally.[10]

During his time in command of 14 Squadron, Buchanan attracted the attentions of a female admirer, Morley Lister, who was the American war correspondent for *Life* magazine. She visited the squadron at Gambut and was impressed with Buchanan's charm, accompanying him on at least two missions – a fact unsurprisingly not recorded in official documents – before a superior in Cairo ordered the unauthorised flights to stop. Nonetheless, the story must have added considerably to Buchanan's growing reputation for eccentricity.

Before he left 14 Squadron in May 1942, Buchanan was awarded a Bar to his DFC, for 'gallantry displayed in flying operations against the enemy'.[11] By 1942 Buchanan had gained a reputation throughout the Middle East for his adventurous, even cavalier, behaviour. He was also known for going up into the air between missions to, in his own words, 'keep his hand in'; such was Buchanan's unremitting love for flying.

During six months of enforced rest in a desk job, he constantly hassled his superiors for an active appointment. Eventually, in November 1942, Buchanan was appointed to command 272 Squadron, based in Malta, and flying Beaufighters. The 272 Squadron had experienced several changes of command in quick succession, after Wing Commander White did not return from a mission on 25 October, and shortly after the temporary commander Squadron Leader Watson was shot down on 14 November. It was perhaps fortunate for the RAF in the Middle East that they had a commander of Buchanan's calibre waiting in the wings.[12]

At this stage in the war Malta was still very much a beleaguered isle. Only in August had the Operation Pedestal convoy run a desperate gauntlet to supply the starving population, and a German and Italian invasion had threatened earlier in 1942.[13] Although the pressure had eased slightly by the time Buchanan arrived, the skies and seas of the Mediterranean still witnessed much fighting. Buchanan's first operation came on 21 November 1942, when he shot down a Heinkel 115 over the Mediterranean. After shooting down the Heinkel, Buchanan carried out a reconnaissance flight over Tunisia, where much fighting was still taking place. The operational tempo in Malta was startling, and Buchanan flew missions in excess of four hours long several days a week, in addition to his duties as commanding officer. Virtually every mission saw Buchanan encounter enemy aircraft. In January 1943 the squadron began operations over Sicily and southern Italy, as Malta became a springboard for attack once the Allies had gained the upper hand in the war in North Africa.[14]

Buchanan had gained a legendary reputation during his time in command of 272 Squadron, and when the squadron was disbanded towards the end of the war, Buchanan was remembered in a very positive manner:

… Wing Commander Buchanan, whose name is a legend throughout the Mediterranean theatre. Every day the Beaus were out intercepting German aircraft passing from Sicily, or strafing the German aerodromes in Tunisia. Later as the Tunisian campaign drew to a close they were transferred to a new and unaccustomed role, that of night intruding over Sicily and Italy. At the same time they continued to escort torpedo 'strikes', to carry out daylight sweeps, to escort convoys and when appropriate indulge in high level dive-bombing on selected targets.[15]

Buchanan's time in Malta was also richly rewarded. In December 1942 Buchanan received yet another award, when he was Mentioned in Despatches.[16] Then in January 1943 Wing Commander Buchanan was awarded the Distinguished Service Order (DSO), which was formally presented by Field Marshal Lord Gort, the Governor of Malta on 24 April.[17] The following citation appeared in the *London Gazette*:

> This officer has participated in a very large number of sorties, involving bombing attacks against many countries occupied by the enemy. He arrived in Malta in November, 1942, and, within the next 14 days, led his squadron in 6 bombing attacks on enemy shipping. During these operations, Wing Commander Buchanan destroyed 6 enemy aircraft in combat. He is a magnificent leader whose great skill and fine fighting qualities have been of incalculable value.

In May 1943 Buchanan was ordered to leave 272 Squadron and take up a staff job with 247 Wing, part of 201 Group. After a hand-over period with his successor, Buchanan left for RAF headquarters in Greece, fittingly in a Beaufighter.[18]

The role of 247 Wing was to be responsible for providing co-operation with the Royal Navy in the eastern Mediterranean, although after such an active posting in Malta, a sedate desk job obviously left the young officer frustrated. However, he soon returned to operational command, when on 17 October 1943 he was given command of 227 Squadron, another Beaufighter unit. Initially based at Lakatamia on Cyprus, the squadron moved to Berka in Libya on 31 November.[19]

After the end of the war in North Africa and the surrender of fascist Italy, the role of the RAF in the Mediterranean changed. Now 227 Squadron was tasked with operations in the seas around Greece, targeting German forces in the area, in particular targeting enemy shipping in the Aegean and providing air cover for Allied convoys. Interestingly, although he took command of the squadron on 17 October, Buchanan did not make his first operational flight until 10 December – strange indeed for an officer who had been hankering for a return to action.

On 16 February 1944 Buchanan led a formation of four aircraft on an offensive sweep in the western Aegean, off the coast of Greece. A successful attack with cannons and bombs was made on a dredger off Mauplia, but Beaufighter EL467 'J', piloted by Buchanan, was struck by light flak in the starboard engine. After attempting to keep it in the air, Buchanan reported over the radio that he would have to ditch into the sea. It appeared to the other aircraft that Buchanan had ditched safely.[20]

What exactly happened to Buchanan after his aircraft crashed has been unclear for some years. However, information held by the RAF's Historical Branch appears to suggest that he was seriously injured when the Beaufighter crash-landed violently. He was last seen floating on a petrol tank that had broken away from the aircraft, waving at a circling aircraft while his observer, Warrant Officer Howes, paddled over to him in a dinghy.

Wing Commander Buchanan was never seen again. Warrant Officer Howes eventually reached land in occupied Greece, and made his was back to Allied territory by 7 April 1944. Buchanan's family were informed that he was missing in action on 24 March, but the news of his loss was not reported in the press for some time in order to protect Howes' safety while he was on the run.[21] When the rest of the formation landed at Berka it was also found that a member of the ground crew, Leading Aircraftsman Eliav, had been on board Buchanan's aircraft as a passenger. He was never seen again after the Beaufighter ditched.

Buchanan had had a remarkable career: in over four years of war he had flown over 800 hours operationally, bombed a staggering thirteen different countries and carried out over 230 missions.[22] These figures are quite staggering for a young officer – it seems that after such a heroic record Buchanan's luck simply ran out.

One of his contemporaries remembered him in glowing terms:

Buck, had he lived in another era, would have been a buccaneer by natural inclination and character. His dandyish outward appearance belied his courage and dash, because he had the guts of a lion when the chips were down. He was one of very few men whom I've always felt highly privileged to have known.[23]

13

Portsmouth's Bomber Boys

IT HAS BECOME one of the peculiarities of the history of the Second World War that the contribution of the RAF's Bomber Command has been overlooked for many years. Whilst the Battle of Britain and Fighter Command have become legendary, the many thousands of men who flew – and died – in bombers have been virtually forgotten. In total, 209 men from Portsmouth are known to have died flying in bomber aircraft during the Second World War. By comparison, only one fighter pilot from Portsmouth died flying during the Battle of Britain.[1]

Early in the war the RAF's bombers were wholly unsuited to undertaking bombing raids over Germany.[2] The first bomber man from Portsmouth to be lost was Sergeant Harry Wakeham, 26 and from Southsea, who died on 2 January 1940. He was serving with 149 Squadron, flying Vickers Wellington Bombers. Wakeham has no known grave, and is remembered on the Runnymede Memorial to the RAF's missing in Surrey.[3]

The bombers were pressed into action attacking ground targets after Germany invaded France, Belgium and Holland in May 1940. Sergeant Alfred Robinson, 26 and from Southsea, and piloting a Blenheim in 40 Squadron, was killed on 10 May 1940 on a raid targeting a military airfield at Ypenburg, where a battle was raging between Dutch and German forces. The aircraft crashed near Voorburg in Holland, and Robinson is buried there. Flight Lieutenant Harold Sammels, 24 and from North End, was killed on 14 May 1940. Flying in a Fairey Battle bomber in 105 Squadron, Sammels' aircraft was lost without trace on a raid targeting Sedan in France, and he is remembered on the Runnymede Memorial. On the same day Sergeant Herbert Trescothic, 25 and from Southsea, who was an observer with 142 Squadron, was killed targeting bridges and roads near Berry-au-Bac. He is buried in Chehery, France. Even after Dunkirk, Bomber Command was still flying missions to attack the Germans in northern France. Sergeant Leslie Keast, 25 and from North End, was killed on 11 June 1940. A pilot with 10 Squadron, Keast was flying a Whitley bomber that crashed near Abbeville, where he is buried. During the late summer of 1940 the RAF was also tasked with bombing German shipping in the Channel ports, which could be used to launch an invasion of Britain. Sergeant Joseph McCormick, 25 and from Southsea, was an observer in a Wellington in 75 (New Zealand) Squadron. It is not known how McCormick's aircraft was lost, but he is buried in Adegem, Belgium.

In 1941 bombers were also tasked with attacking German warships sheltering in French ports. On 24 July 1941 Flight Sergeant Charles Horner, 30 and from Paulsgrove, was the observer in a Halifax in 76 Squadron, and tasked with attacking the German battleship *Scharnhorst* at La Pallice. Horner's aircraft is believed to have been shot down near L'Aiguillon-sur-Mer in France, where Horner and the rest of the crew are buried.

On 27 July 1942 Wing Commander Frank Dixon-Wright, 31 and from Southsea, was killed during a raid on Hamburg. The commanding officer of 115 Squadron, his Wellington was lost in the North Sea, and Dixon-Wright is remembered on the Runnymede Memorial. Dixon-Wright had been awarded the DFC in September 1941 for attacks on the German warships *Gneisenau*, *Scharnhorst* and *Prinz Eugen* at Brest and La Pallice. These raids were in daylight and faced extremely heavy flak and fighter defences.[4]

The bomber offensive intensified after Air Chief Marshal Sir Arthur 'Bomber' Harris became commander in chief of Bomber Command.[5] In March 1943 Harris began targeting the Ruhr industrial region, in what became known as the Battle of the Ruhr. Between March and July 1943, nineteen Portsmouth men were lost targeting industrial towns and cities, such as Emmerich, Dortmund, Essen, Dusseldorf, Bochum, Cologne, Krefeld, Mullheim and Wuppertal.

One young man in particular distinguished himself during the Battle of the Ruhr, and his experiences also give us a valuable insight into service in Bomber Command. Sergeant Francis Cyril Compton, 20 and from Paulsgrove, was the son of Charles Edgar and Elsie Beatrice Compton. After joining the Portsmouth Electricity Service on 14 February 1940, Francis Compton joined the RAF not long afterwards.[6] After passing through 4th Air Gunners School at Morpeth, 24th Operational Training Unit at Heneybourne and then 1658th Operational Conversion Unit at Ricall,[7] Compton was posted to 10 Squadron as a rear gunner on 24 March 1943.[8] Air gunners were traditionally the lowest ranking aircrew, and the rear gunner's position was notorious for being exposed and vulnerable to flak.[9]

Compton's first raid came on 2 April, on the French port of L'Orient, and his first major raid on Germany came two days later, as part of an operation targeting the German port of Kiel. Six days later they were bombing Frankfurt, and later, on 10 April, they bombed Stuttgart. On this occasion the bomb doors failed to open over the target and the bomb load was jettisoned on the way home. Two nights later they took part in a disastrous raid on the Škoda Motor Works in the Czech town of Pilsen, where navigational errors led to only one bomber out of the 327 actually hitting the target.[10] Four days later they were sent on another long trip to the Polish city of Stettin, on the Baltic coast. This time the 339 aircraft caused severe damage, although 6.9 per cent of the aircraft were lost.[11]

After a lull of more than a week, 572 bombers were sent to Duisburg on the night of 12 May,[12] and it was on this occasion that Compton first distinguished himself in action. On the return leg, 20 miles east of Arnhem in Holland, their Halifax, JD947, was attacked by a Messerschmitt 110.[13] The tail and bomb doors were hit and two of the fuel tanks were holed. Compton returned fire, causing the Me110 to rear up and dive away. Later, over The Hague, an Me109 was spotted by Compton, who instructed the pilot to take violent evasive action to port. They finally landed their battered Halifax at 4.29 a.m.

The crew had very little respite, however, and the very next night they were sent to bomb Bochum. Taking off at 11.55 p.m. in HR695, their replacement aircraft, the crew were spotted by searchlights between Dusseldorf and Cologne. The pilot took evasive action, but a flak burst caused their aircraft to spin over on to its back and fall to 7,000ft. By a remarkable piece of flying, the pilot managed to right the aircraft, but the mid-upper gunner was found to be missing. Their ordeal was not over, however, as they were again 'coned' by searchlights, before deciding to make for home. Over south Beveland, Compton sighted two Junkers 88s and fired at one, while the other overshot. The pilot took evasive action but both returned. Compton again returned fire, before seeing smoke appear from one of the enemy aircraft's engines. The Halifax escaped, but was heavily damaged – the port tail plane, elevator, rudder and port outer tank were all damaged with bullet holes.[14]

For his bravery over Duisburg and Bochum, Compton was awarded the Distinguished Flying Medal (DFM). The award was announced in the *London Gazette* on 4 June 1943 with the following citation:

> One night in May, 1943, this airman was the rear gunner of an aircraft detailed to attack Duisburg. During the operation his aircraft was attacked and damaged by an enemy fighter. Sergeant Compton resolutely returned fire and, following an accurate burst, the enemy aircraft stalled and then fell towards the ground, disappearing out of sight through the clouds. Half an hour later, the bomber was again attacked by enemy fighters. In the ensuing action Sergeant Compton coolly and skilfully used his guns while giving his captain directions which enabled him to evade the attackers. The following night during an operation against Bochum his aircraft which had been damaged by anti-aircraft fire, was attacked by two enemy aircraft. Displaying great skill and determination, Sergeant Compton shot one of them down. Although his guns were rendered useless, he gave his captain a commentary which enabled him to evade the remaining fighter. On both occasions this airman displayed great courage and determination and contributed materially to the safe return of the aircraft.[15]

Compton and his comrades were given a well-deserved respite before their next operation over Dortmund on 23 May 1943. They also had a new mid-upper gunner. The sortie was not a complete success, however, as one of their bombs hung up in the bomb rack and had to be jettisoned on the return journey. Two nights later they took part in a raid of 759 aircraft on Dusseldorf, and then on 29 May they were part of a large force that targeted Wuppertal, in one of the most successful raids during the Battle of the Ruhr.

In a short space of time Compton and his colleagues had flown eleven sorties with 10 Squadron, and had distinguished themselves in the process. On 2 June 1943, Compton and the rest of his crew were transferred to 35 Squadron, part of Bomber Command's elite Pathfinder Force. After several weeks of settling in and training they began active operations with the Pathfinders on 19 June.[16]

Compton and his crew took off on a raid over Cologne on 29 June 1943. Piloted by Sergeant Beveridge, Halifax HR812 'F for Freddie' took off from Gravely in Cambridgeshire at 11.27 p.m. The aircraft is believed to have been shot down by a night fighter, piloted by Lieutenant Heinz-Wolfgang Schnaufer. Schnaufer was the Luftwaffe's most successful night-fighter ace, with 121 kills. The Halifax crashed at Wandre, 8km north-east of Liege,

Belgium. Along with Compton, the pilot, flight engineer and mid gunner were also killed. The air bomber, Sergeant Billet, evaded immediate capture but was taken prisoner in Bordeaux. The three other crew members survived but were captured at the scene. Compton is buried in a collective grave along with his comrades in Heverlee War Cemetery, Belgium, thus ending the very short but brave career of a young Portsmouth airman.

After the end of the Battle of the Ruhr, Bomber Command was given a vital mission to hinder the development of one of Nazi Germany's secret weapons. On 18 August 1943 three Portsmouth airmen were lost during Operation Hydra, the costly raid on the German rocket development site at Peenemunde on the Baltic coast.[17] Sergeant Arthur Purrington, of 49 Squadron, was shot down over the Baltic in his Lancaster. He has no known grave and is remembered on the Runnymede Memorial. Sergeant Cyril Williams, 33 and from Copnor, was the navigator in a Lancaster PM-P in 103 Squadron. The aircraft crashed near Flensburg on the Danish border, and Williams is buried in Kiel War Cemetery. Sergeant Dennis Carrington, 21 and from Cosham, was the wireless operator in a Stirling EF47 in 620 Squadron. Carrington's aircraft is believed to have been shot down by the joint efforts of flak and a night fighter, crashing at Wusterhusen, and he is buried in Berlin 1939-1945 War Cemetery.

Shortly after the raid on Peenemunde, Bomber Harris turned his attention to Berlin.[18] The subsequent offensive exacted a heavy toll on Allied aircrews and it became known as 'Bomber Command's Passchendaele'. More men from Portsmouth were killed raiding Berlin than any other target during the Second World War, totalling fifteen men between November 1943 and March 1944. The first losses came on 22 November 1943, the second major raid of the battle. Pilot Officer Geoffrey Stokes, 21 and from Milton, was flying a Lancaster in 156 Squadron and was lost without trace. Sergeant John Whitehead of Southsea was flying in a Halifax in 51 Squadron and is believed to have crashed in the Ijselmeer, a large inland lake in Holland. Both Stokes and Whitehead are remembered on the Runnymede Memorial.

Night after night the bombers returned to what the crews called the 'big city'. Heavy casualties were experienced on 29 January 1944 and two Portsmouth men were among them. Sergeant Norman Vincent, 22, was flying in a Lancaster in 97 Squadron and was lost without trace. Flight Lieutenant Dennis Woodruff, 28 and from North End, was flying in a Lancaster in 15 Squadron and was also lost without trace. Vincent and Woodruff are both remembered on the Runnymede Memorial. Woodruff was awarded a posthumous DFC, which was announced in the *London Gazette* on 11 February 1944:[19]

As captain of aircraft Flight Lieutenant Woodruff has participated in a large number of sorties, including attacks on such targets as Berlin, Hamburg and Turin. On one occasion, whilst over Kassel, his aircraft was attacked by a fighter. Although much damage was sustained, Flight Lieutenant Woodruff skilfully manoeuvred his aircraft to enable his gunner to fire a long burst of fire at the attacker which went down in flames. Flight Lieutenant Woodruff then went on to complete a successful attack on the target. This officer has invariably displayed great courage and determination.

On 24 March 1944 one of the last major raids on Berlin resulted in the loss of three Portsmouth airmen. Sergeant Oscar Sporne, 20 and from Cosham, was the flight engineer in a Halifax in 433 Squadron and was brought down by flak on the homeward journey. Sergeant Norman

Cooper, aged 24, was flying in a Halifax in 640 Squadron and is believed to have crashed, although the exact site is unknown. Sergeant Norman Lowlett was the flight engineer in a Halifax in 578 Squadron, which was shot down by flak north of Erfurt. Sporne, Cooper and Lowlett are all buried in Berlin 1939–1945 War Cemetery.

As Operation Overlord loomed in 1944, Bomber Command was switched to attacking transportation targets in France, as part of a plan to disrupt German reinforcements to the battle area once the invasion began.[20] The first Portsmouth airman to be lost during this phase of the air war was Flight Sergeant George Evans, 23 and from North End, who was an air bomber in a Lancaster in 50 Squadron. Evans' aircraft was tasked with bombing a military camp at Mailly-le-Camp in France and, although it is not known how the aircraft was lost, he is buried in Marigny-en-Orxois, France. On 9 May Sergeant Leslie Lewis, the wireless operator in a Lancaster in 35 Squadron, was lost on a raid to bomb railway yards at Hainne St Pierr. Lewis' aircraft crashed near Mons in Belgium, and he is buried in Chievres, Belgium. Several nights later, on the 11th, bombers were sent to attack a military camp at Bourg-Leopold in Belgium. Pilot Officer Leslie Watson, 23 and from Hilsea, was the wireless operator in a Lancaster in 467 (Australian) Squadron. The aircraft was picked up by a night fighter over the target and was seen to explode in flames. Watson is buried in Leopoldsburg War Cemetery, Belgium. The next night Sergeant Peter Rowthorn, 19 and from Copnor, was killed over Bourg-Leopold, Belgium. Part of the crew in a Lancaster in 630 Squadron, Rowthorn was shot down by a night fighter over Antwerp, and is buried in Schoonselhof War Cemetery, Belgium.

Only a matter of days before D-Day, one Portsmouth airman was lost bombing one of the major threats to the invasion. Flight Sergeant Harry O'Bree was lost during the mission on 28 May 1944 to bomb the Merville Gun Battery, which threatened the east flank of the Allied beachhead. An air bomber with 460 (Australian) Squadron, O'Bree's Lancaster was lost off the French coast, and he is remembered on the Runnymede Memorial. After D-Day, bombers were also called in to support operations on the ground, and on 18 July hundreds of bombers targeted the battle area around Caen. Flight Sergeant Kenneth Meehan, 20 and from North End, was the navigator of a Halifax in 158 Squadron which crashed near the target. Meehan is buried in Banneville-la-Campagne War Cemetery. Also lost on the same day was Sergeant Keith Burrows, aged 19, who was flying in a Lancaster in 44 Squadron when it was shot down over the target area. Burrows has no known grave and is remembered on the Runnymede Memorial.

After the Battle of Normandy the bombers were allowed to return to targets in Germany. Flight Lieutenant Patrick McCarthy, 21 and from Southsea, was killed on the night of 18/19 August 1944 when his Lancaster PB148 in 7 Squadron crashed. He and his crew, serving as pathfinders, were on a mission to bomb Sterkrade, a synthetic oil-processing plant near Oberhausen in the Ruhr. McCarthy's aircraft 'C for Charlie' was the only aircraft lost in the war known to have contained two Portsmouth men. Also on board was Pilot Officer Alan Hargrave, 24, who was a navigator.

Patrick McCarthy originally served as a warrant officer, before being commissioned as an officer on 8 April 1944. It seems that he and his crew had served in bombers and been transferred to the pathfinders, in the same manner as Francis Compton. McCarthy and his crew first flew with 7 Squadron on 25 February 1944 on a raid over Augsburg. For the next few months they took part in raids on Stuttgart, Frankfurt and Berlin, before moving to targets in

Flight Lieutenant Patrick
McCarthy DFC in flying gear.
(Chrissie Lynn)

No. 7 Squadron,
Royal Air Force,
Oakington,
Cambridge.

7S/3260/30/P1.   16th. September, 1944.

Dear Mrs. McCarthy,

It gives me great pleasure to inform
you that His Majesty the King has approved
the award of the Distinguished Flying Cross
to your son, Acting Flight Lieutenant
P.G. McCarthy.

We on the Squadron know how truly well-
earned is this award, and repeat our whole-
hearted wishes for his safety in order that he
may soon personally receive this coveted
award.

Yours sincerely,

[signature] F/L
Adjutant

Mrs. J.McCarthy,
17, Havelock Road,
Southsea, Hants.

A letter sent by the adjutant of
7 Squadron to Patrick McCarthy's mother
after he was lost in action. *(Chrissie Lynn)*

The Runnymede Memorial records the names of more than 20,000 airmen lost during the Second World War who have no known grave. *(Steve Poole, Flickr user Stavioni)*

northern France in preparation for the D-Day landings. On the eve of D-Day McCarthy and his crew bombed the Merville Gun Battery, which was then stormed by airborne forces in the early hours of D-Day itself. Raids on French targets continued throughout June and July 1944, before Bomber Command was allowed to turn their attention back to Germany. Sorties on Kiel and Stuttgart were interspersed with more missions over France, including a raid in direct support of ground troops on 30 July. Meanwhile, Alan Hargrave, who had originally served as a flight sergeant, was commissioned as a pilot officer and then made an acting flight lieutenant in rapid succession. On several raids in July and August 1944 McCarthy acted as deputy master bomber, a crucial role in co-ordinating a raid involving hundreds of aircraft.[21]

Bomber Command records state only that 'C for Charlie' took off from RAF Oakington at 11.04 p.m. – no other information is available. Records do state, however, that MG-C had eight crew members on board, although Lancasters normally only had seven men. Was the extra man a rookie flying for experience or was his presence something more sinister? Crew lists suggest that there were two air bombers on board, which adds to the likelihood that one of them was a rookie from another crew who had gone along for the experience. It appears that when the aircraft crashed near Alkmaar in Holland the Germans may have mistook the extra man for a spy and subsequently killed all of the crew as spies. McCarthy, Hargrave and the rest of their crew are buried in Bergen War Cemetery, Holland. Their fate was not known until after the end of the war, but there is no evidence that the incident was investigated as a war crime. Patrick McCarthy was posthumously awarded the DFC, announced in the *London Gazette* on 15 September 1944.

No Portsmouth men are known to have taken part in the famous Dambusters Raid in 1943, but in October 1944 one young Portsmouth airman was killed flying with 617 Squadron, the famous Dambusters. Flight Sergeant Herbert Clarke, 22 and from Mile End, was an air gunner in Lancaster LM482. On an operation targeting the Kembs Dam, the aircraft's Tallboy bomb failed to release and the crew turned away for a second run-in. They were hit by flak and crashed at Efringen-Kirchen, a village just inside Germany near the Swiss border. Clarke was Mentioned in Despatches during his career, and is buried in Durnbach War Cemetery, Germany.

The last Portsmouth bomber boy to die in action over Germany was Sergeant Edward Ford, a 20-year-old flight engineer from Mile End. Ford was flying in a Lancaster in 50 Squadron on a daylight raid on oil storage tanks in the Hamburg area on 9 April 1945. Ford's aircraft crashed in the target area, and he is buried in Hamburg War Cemetery, Germany.

By the end of the war some 55,500 bomber crew had been lost. Flying with Bomber Command presented poor odds of survival: in 1943 only 17 per cent of crews lasted a tour of thirty operations unscathed, while overall only 24 per cent of aircrew survived the war unharmed.[22] By comparison, such a scale of losses would have been considered catastrophic in an infantry battalion. That so many young men steeled themselves against these stark odds and went up into the sky night after night makes the bomber offensive one of the most sobering campaigns of the Second World War. Sadly, although the effectiveness of Bomber Command's strategic-bombing offensive has been debated, history has long neglected the sacrifice of these brave young men.

14

'Nine Gun': Flight Lieutenant John Coghlan DFC

THE MEN OF Fighter Command who took part in the Battle of Britain have gone down in history as the 'few'. One man in particular was even 'fewer', as he became the only Portsmouth fighter pilot to die in action in the summer of 1940. Not only was John Coghlan unique in this respect, but his fighting record and character encapsulated perfectly the spirit of the men who defended Britain in the sky. His death in suspicious circumstances only adds to the mystery surrounding a remarkable man.

John Hunter Coghlan was born in Shanghai, China, on 7 September 1914, the son of Henry Hunter Coghlan and Katherine Coghlan.[1] Between May 1927 and July 1933 Coghlan attended Imperial Service College, a school in Windsor for the children of army officers. After leaving the Imperial Service College, Coghlan also attended Portsmouth Grammar School, as his family originally came from Southsea. In 1939 his mother was recorded as living in Worthing Road,[2] and his aunt Beatrice Bouchier is also known to have lived in Southsea.[3]

John Coghlan joined the RAF in January 1936, making his first training flight on 4 February 1936 in a Tiger Moth trainer. His first solo flight came just over two weeks later, on 19 February.[4] After initial flight training at 7th Flying Training School in Peterborough, he was commissioned in October 1936[5] as an acting pilot officer. After initially serving with 1 (Fighter) Squadron at Tangmere in Sussex, Coghlan was promoted, in March 1937, to pilot officer and posted to 72 Squadron, also at Tangmere.[6] By July 1937, 72 Squadron had moved to RAF Church Fenton, a new airfield in Yorkshire that had opened in April of the same year as part of the RAF's pre-war expansion programme.

In May 1938 Coghlan was posted back to 1(F) Squadron, who were still at Tangmere.[7] On 20 October Coghlan made his first flight in a Hurricane, a new aircraft that was reaching fighter squadrons in increasing numbers, and by November 1938 he had been promoted to flying officer.[8] In February 1939 he had been posted to 56 Squadron, who were based at RAF North Weald in Essex, which was one of the few modern all-weather airfields in Fighter Command, with a macadam runway; many fighter airfields still had grass dispersal areas and runways.

Flight Lieutenant John
Coghlan DFC and
other 56 Squadron
aircrew. Coghlan
is in the back row,
third from the right,
sporting a moustache.
(www.acesofww2.com)

Coghlan was still serving with 56 Squadron, part of Fighter Command's 11 Group, when war was declared in September 1939, and he had amassed a total of 606 flying hours on a variety of aircraft types by this time.[9] The squadron was equipped with Hawker Hurricane single-seat fighters.

Early in the war 56 Squadron was involved in a tragic incident, the Battle of Barking Creek. On 6 September 1939 two Hurricanes of 56 Squadron took off from North Weald on a scramble and were wrongly identified as enemy aircraft. Spitfires were despatched from Hornchurch to intercept them and both Hurricanes were shot down, killing Pilot Officer Montague Hulton-Harrop. This tragedy shows just how dangerous aerial combat could be, even during an apparently quiet phase of the war.[10]

After fears of an immediate German offensive subsided, the early months of the war were spent on routine patrols, training flights and reconnaissance. As the winter weather set in flying was seriously curtailed and little was seen of the Luftwaffe, apart from the odd enemy aircraft requiring interception missions.[11] There were also occasional shipping convoy escort duties.

With the onset of spring, however, Coghlan found himself flying more patrols, some lasting for several hours, and when not on operational missions pilots also carried on training, including taking new pilots up in dual-controlled aircraft. The squadron also practised night flying, low-level flying, formation flying and interceptions.[12]

Eric Clayton, a mechanic with 56 Squadron, remembered his first impressions of John Coghlan:

> He was a short, heavily built man with dark hair brushed straight back and a large moustache. He was a friendly, amusing and unflappable character; overweight and unfit, he perspired freely and had a prodigious intake of ale. He ran a long, low Jaguar and had an unmarried partner. I came to know and respect him.[13]

A photograph of Coghlan with some of his 56 Squadron colleagues confirms Clayton's impressions. Coghlan appears every inch the young fighter pilot, with broad shoulders, a trademark RAF moustache, brylcreem-style hair and looking much older than his 26 years. Clayton's remarks about Coghlan's intake of ale are not untypical of Fighter Command airmen – most accounts suggest that they fought hard during the day and played hard in the local pubs at night.

The coming of war had brought frenzied preparations to North Weald. The men lived in tents, and were served meals by the wives and girlfriends of the pilots – including Coghlan's unmarried partner. According to Eric Clayton, Coghlan and his partner could often be encountered on a night out in the pubs of nearby Ipswich. Officer pilots did not normally socialise with their ground crew, but Clayton suggests that Coghlan was an exception and was relaxed about mixing with other ranks.

Thankfully we have first-hand evidence of the fighting that John Coghlan took part in during 1940. Aerial combat reports were completed by all Fighter Command pilots after any flight in which they had encountered the enemy, and a number of reports completed by John Coghlan are in the National Archives. They do not represent all of the times on which Coghlan saw action; nevertheless, the following accounts do give a vivid impression of the intensity of air combat in the summer of 1940.

On 9 May 1940 three Hurricanes of Red Section, 56 Squadron, were led on a patrol by Coghlan 15 miles east of Clacton, Essex, when a Junkers 88 was spotted. The Ju88 climbed some distance, made a stalled turn and then dived at great speed. Coghlan and his colleagues were unable to get within effective range, and although Coghlan expended all of his ammunition in one burst at 500 to 600 yards, no damage was caused. The enemy aircraft's rear gunner fired at Coghlan, but no bullets struck his aircraft. Coghlan returned to North Weald while his number two and number three continued the chase, which they broke off 50 miles out into the North Sea.[14]

The Germans launched their invasion of France and the Low Countries the next day, on 10 May, and Coghan spent more than four hours of that day patrolling the skies over southern England. For much of the following month the squadron were operating from Biggin Hill, London, and Manston, Kent. On 16 May the squadron was sent to France,[15] and shortly before their departure Coghlan was promoted to flight lieutenant and transferred to command 'A' Flight. On 17 May Coghlan provided an escort to Abbeville, and he spent the next few weeks flying over southern England, the Channel and northern France.

On 18 May 1940, 56 Squadron's 'A' Flight and aircraft from 213 Squadron encountered eight Messerschmitt 109s over Mauberge, France. The enemy aircraft approached from the right at 5,000ft, and Coghlan tried to warn the rest of the formation but his radio would not work. The sky became full of aircraft and a frenetic dogfight ensued. Coghlan attacked a Me109 that was on the tail of two Hurricanes, firing a three-second burst. After making a right-hand turn he saw another three Me109s on the tail of a Hurricane, so he fired a ten to twelve-second burst at the rear 109 and saw it disappear. He returned to the squadron's airfield from the direction of Boulogne.[16]

The next day 'A' Flight was on patrol over Lille in northern France. Coghlan became separated from his colleagues, and then noticed Hurricanes, which he thought belonged to his squadron. He then noticed a 'black burst' in the sky, and twelve to fifteen Heinkel 111s at 12,000ft, though he does not mention in his combat report exactly what the black burst was. Coghlan approached on a rapid climb and engaged the left-hand 111. He saw explosions in the fuselage, shortly followed by the port and starboard engines. He then broke away after expending his ammunition, and the formation of Heinkels broke up.[17]

On 27 May the entire squadron encountered ten 111s at 10,000ft over Ostend, Belgium. Coghlan attacked the right-hand Heinkel, firing a five-second burst at 100 yards, and then another two five-second bursts at even closer range, before seeing the enemy aircraft's fuselage burst into flames. As the Heinkel fell out of formation Pilot Officer Fisher also attacked the stricken aircraft and it went down in flames. As Coghlan was out of ammunition he returned to RAF Manston, an airfield on the east coast of Kent from which 56 Squadron was operating.[18]

As the British army was being compressed into a small pocket around Dunkirk, the air battle over northern France intensified. On 27 May eight Hurricanes of 56 Squadron were on patrol over Dunkirk and encountered forty to fifty Messerschmitt 109s. Coghlan, at around 2,000ft, initially spotted ten Me110s at a lower height, and then was warned over the radio that there were more enemy aircraft above. Five enemy aircraft converged on him from above, and Coghlan climbed to attack, firing at the leader. Afterwards he attacked one of the lower flying fighters and, after using the last of his ammunition, dived with three enemy aircraft on his tail.[19]

Two days later Coghlan and 56 Squadron were again in action over the beaches of Dunkirk. After leaving Manston at 7.15 p.m., 56 Squadron patrolled the beach along with 151 and two other squadrons. Shortly after arriving they spotted a lone Ju88 with fifty Me109s above. Coghlan and his section climbed to attack, and two of the fighters passed in front of him at extremely close range. He opened fire with two bursts of five seconds each, hitting both enemy aircraft, and their engines began giving off white smoke.[20]

During and after the Dunkirk evacuation it was frequently commented by soldiers that the RAF was nowhere to be seen, but Coghlan's reports are testimony to the bitter fighting that was taking place in the skies above Dunkirk's sand dunes. The fighter pilots were fighting very hard indeed. During one engagement over France, Coghlan had extinguished all of his ammunition. Undeterred, he proceeded to empty his Smith and Wesson pistol at the enemy aircraft. After this incident he became known as 'Nine Gun' Coghlan, because most RAF fighters at the time only had eight machine guns. Although this incident has comedy value, it also shows a real determination to get to grips with the enemy by any means.

On 31 May, 56 Squadron flew to Digby for a well-earned rest, with 111 Squadron taking over at North Weald. The rest was short-lived, however, as they transferred back to North Weald on 4 June. Two days later the squadron flew via Hawkinge to patrol over Abbeville and Amiens, landing at Rouen before returning home. Much of the next few weeks were spent flying from southern England to patrol or escort bombers over the battlefields in northern France.

After the evacuation at Dunkirk there seems to have been a relative lull in air activity, as Coghlan's next aerial combat report was not until 3 July 1940. Red Section was scrambled to intercept an incoming enemy aircraft, but one of the Hurricanes became lost in cloud. The remaining two were directed to Felixstowe, and Coghlan caught sight of a Dornier 215 bomber over Orford Ness. As his radio was out of service, Coghlan rocked his wings to catch his wingman's attention. The two Hurricanes took turns to fire bursts at the Dornier, and when they finally lost sight its port engine and wing were on fire. Coghlan was fired on by the bomber but not hit. It is believed that the Dornier crashed into the sea off Burham and that its intended target was RAF Manston.[21]

On 10 July 'A' Flight were in action to defend a coastal convoy that had come under attack 10 miles south of Lydd in the English Channel. Dorniers and Heinkels were bombing the ships, escorted by Me109 and Me110 fighters. An intense dogfight ensued, in which Coghlan began by chasing a 110, but then had to evade two 109s. He then attacked another 110, and the enemy aircraft's port wing and engine burst into flames, before falling out of the sky. Coghlan then became aware of 109s behind him, as red cannon fire shot past the cockpit. He pulled up and throttled back, and the 109s shot beneath him. He then managed to dive down on them, giving each a three-second burst at 50 yards' range. Coghlan was then attacked by another 109, but escaped damage. The attack on the convoy had been broken up.[22]

Three days later Coghlan was again in action, this time off the coast of Calais, flying with 'B' Flight. Nine to twelve Junkers 87 'Stukas' were sighted crossing the French coast, and Red Section formed into a line and went into attack, forcing the Stukas to drop their bombs into the sea and dive to sea level. After the Hurricanes attacked, one Stuka flew straight into the sea. Heinkel 113s then came in to attack, and Coghlan had to outmanoeuvre several, shaking off his attackers before firing at a Heinkel that was attacking his Hurricane from astern. The Heinkel turned right and smashed into the sea. After a prolonged melee the 113s disappeared; there had been several splashes in the sea.[23]

For his prolonged bravery in action during the summer of 1940, Flight Lieutenant Coghlan was recommended for the DFC, which was announced in the *London Gazette* on 30 July 1940:

> Awarded the Distinguished Flying Cross. Acting Flight Lieutenant John Hunter COGHLAN (37719). This officer has been a flight commander in his squadron on most of the recent patrols and has led the squadron on some occasions. At all times he has shown the greatest initiative and courage and has personally destroyed at least six enemy aircraft.[24]

Coghlan had shown great courage during the Battle of France and the early part of the Battle of Britain, and had shown great leadership skills in command of a section and then a flight. He was officially credited with destroying at least six enemy aircraft, and by early August had flown over 200 hours in the eleven months since the start of the war.[25] To give an impression of the intensity of the fighting in the spring and summer of 1940, Coghlan fired a total of 189,446 machine gun rounds between 18 May, when he fired his first shots, and 3 August, when he left the squadron. In the same period 56 Squadron had lost nine pilots killed or missing.[26] While the Battle of Britain was still at its height, however, his career was to take a dramatic turn.

Coghlan's last flight with 56 Squadron was on 3 August 1940. The 56 Squadron's operational record book recorded on 5 August that he was being transferred, and two days later Flight Lieutenant Coghlan arrived at the Parachute Practice Unit at Ringway, Manchester.[27] Ringway was responsible for training RAF personnel in using parachutes, and had also recently become the centre for training new army commando units in parachuting. Special Operations Executive establishments trained special agents, and it was probably for this reason that Coghlan was posted to Ringway in August 1940. Aircrew who had served a long tour on operations would be rotated to other duties, although given that the Battle of Britain was at its height in August and Fighter Command was desperately short of aircrew, it is intriguing that such an experienced pilot was allowed to leave. It is likely that Coghlan had volunteered for special duties – perhaps he was looking for a new challenge.

At Ringway Coghlan learnt to fly the Westland Lysander. The Lysander was a light aircraft, perfectly suited for the clandestine business of transporting special agents to and from occupied Europe. Prior to volunteering for special duties, Coghlan's log book shows that he had flown a mere thirty minutes in a Lysander back in January 1939.[28] Later in the war this task would be performed by several special duties squadrons flying Lysanders, but in 1940 the Special Operations Executive was still in its infancy – indeed, it had only been formed in July and its first organised network in France was not started until 1941. Therefore special operations flights were still very much on an ad hoc basis, and records of the flights that did take place are virtually non-existent.

On 17 August 1940 Coghlan took off in Lysander 'C' of the Parachute Practice Unit. He was performing a special duties flight and was carrying an unidentified passenger, believed to be a special agent. His former mechanic, Eric Clayton, recalled seeing Coghlan at Manston before he took off on this clandestine mission:

> A stocky figure in white flying overalls was followed by a smallish man wearing a brown leather jacket and black beret. It was F/L Coghlan DFC and his passenger who was a Frenchman. We were both pleasantly surprised to see each other, for we had had little contact since his transfer to A Flight and none since his posting from 56. He introduced me to his passenger, who said little, and then inevitably the question arose, 'What are you doing here'? From his guarded remarks, it was clear that he was going to drop his passenger into France who, it was equally clear, was an agent.[29]

There is uncertainty about what exactly happened to Coghlan and his passenger. Some sources, including his former mechanic Eric Clayton, state that they were captured in northern France and were executed by the Germans. Other sources suggest that they were either shot down or crashed in the Channel and their bodies were recovered. During the war his fate was unknown, and he was only declared missing presumed killed in action on 21 September. He was finally declared deceased on 17 February 1942,[30] but it was only after the end of the war that his grave was found in France.

Local sources appear to suggest that Coghlan's body was washed ashore at Wimereux, several miles from Boulogne. He is buried in Boulougne Eastern Cemetery in northern France.

Had Coghlan survived, it is likely that an airman with his character and record might have progressed even further within the RAF. And had he remained with Fighter Command during the Battle of Britain, he might well have gained more than the six kills that he had to his credit. Having commanded flights – and on occasions led the whole squadron – in action, he could have looked forward to commanding his own squadron in due course.

15

Brothers in Arms: The Venables Brothers

PERHAPS ONE OF the saddest incidents in the Second World War involving Portsmouth men took part after formal hostilities had actually ended. The sad story of Arthur and Guy Venables is also possibly one of very few instances in which brothers were killed whilst on board the same aircraft. Flying Officer Arthur Venables, aged 23, was a pilot with 78 Squadron, and his brother, Flying Officer Guy Venables, aged 21, was his bomb aimer. Arthur and Guy both hailed from Hilsea, the sons of Ernest and Kate Venables.

Percy Harding-Morris met Guy Venables while he was training at the Blackburn Aircraft Factory in Brough, east Yorkshire, learning to fly on Tiger Moths. Guy Venables became a good friend of the Harding-Morris family and was a frequent visitor to their home in Brough.[1] The friendship of a local family must have been of great comfort to a young man far from home during wartime.

It must have been extremely rare for two brothers to be flying in the same aircraft. Aircrews – in particular bomber crews – were formed in a very organic way, by the simple expedient of placing the required number of men of each role in a room and letting them 'crew-up' of their own accord. Therefore it is remarkable that the Venables brothers must have found themselves progressing through training at the same time. That the Venables brothers flew together is even more unusual when we consider that they both arrived at 78 Squadron on 20 January 1945, but from different directions – Arthur from 75 Base Unit and Guy from 74 Base Unit.[2]

The brothers flew their first mission on 1 February 1945, on a bombing raid to Mainz, Germany. The Venables brothers were perhaps fortunate that they had joined Bomber Command during the final phase of the war against Germany, when the Allies had complete air superiority and Allied bombers encountered less and less in the way of air defences. They flew a total of eighteen missions between February 1945 and the cessation of strategic bombing at the end of April 1945. Their missions took them to targets such as Cologne, Hamburg, Dortmund, Wuppertal and also 'gardening' missions dropping mines in German coastal waters. The German defences were so weak by 1945 that several of these missions were during daylight – something that would have been unthinkable only a year previously. For example, on 12 March 1945 a raid on Dortmund took off at 1.18 p.m. and landed at 7.14 p.m., and a mission to Wuppertal the next day took off at 12.53 p.m. and returned to base at 6.43 p.m.

Guy Venables was principally a bomb aimer, but on several occasions squadron records suggest that he swapped roles with the crew's navigator. This was not usual, but unsurprising given that the training for navigators and bomb aimers was not dissimilar, involving a large degree of map reading and plotting. In fact, the aiming of bombs had originally been part of the navigator's role.[3]

With the drawing down of the strategic bombing of Germany as the war drew to a close, there was less of a need for large bombers, although there was a greater demand for transport aircraft. No 4 Group, Bomber Command was transferred in its entirety to Transport Command with effect from 7 May 1945. In June the squadron began training for the transport role with their Halifaxs, pending a conversion to operating the C-47 Dakota, the military version of the famous Douglas DC-3. On 15 June 78 Squadron was informed that it was to be transferred to the Far East, to join the war effort against Japan, which was expected to last for some time yet. In July the first Dakotas began arriving, and the men were given a round of vaccinations.

With the dropping of the atomic bombs on Japan in August 1945, however, the war in the Far East ended far sooner than expected. It was probably this unexpected development which led to 78 Squadron being transferred to the Middle East instead, and the squadron began moving on 4 September 1945. The Venables brothers took off carrying a number of ground crew in their Dakota, with Arthur as pilot and Guy now acting as his co-pilot. They could have been excused for hoping that flying transport aircraft during peacetime would be a relatively safe posting.

The journey to the Middle East required a number of stops, in order for aircrew to rest and the aircraft to be refuelled, and it was during one of these stops that tragedy struck. On 5 September 1945 the Venables' Dakota KP235 landed at Istres in southern France. The aircraft later attempted to take off at night in poor visibility – squadron records state the aircraft's take-off time as 3.10 a.m., and that there was a thick mist at the end of the runway. The pilot, Arthur Venables, is thought to have seen the mist and pulled the aircraft's nose up sharply, thinking it was high ground. The engine stalled and, with insufficient height to recover, the Dakota struck the ground.[4]

Sixteen men were killed instantly, including thirteen ground crew who were being transported, one man died of his injuries the next day and seven men escaped with injuries. The men killed in the crash, including Arthur and Guy Venables, are buried in Mazargues War Cemetery, southern France.[5] Furthermore, their father Ernest sadly passed away in late 1945 at the age of 54, only a matter of weeks after the death of his sons.[6] Raymond Harding-Morris later visited their mother, Kate Venables, while he was serving in the Fleet Air Arm at HMS *Daedalus* in Lee-on-the-Solent.[7]

It was an extremely sad and tragic end for two men, who had flown eighteen missions over occupied Europe during the last phase of the war only to be killed in a peacetime accident. Although the world was now at peace, there were still millions of men in uniform, and flying was still a dangerous occupation. The Venables brothers must have been among the very few – perhaps the only – brothers to die together flying with the RAF during the Second World War. Their family must have suffered a considerable shock to lose two sons at the same time in such a tragic manner.

PART FOUR
THE OTHER SERVICES

16

The NAAFI

LOSSES DURING WARTIME were by no means confined to servicemen and women: a large number of civilians were killed while on active service during the Second World War. A significant number of them were working for the NAAFI, the Navy, Army and Air Force Institute.

The Navy, Army and Air Force Institute was founded in 1921 after the experience of the First World War, when a range of canteens were provided to support men at the front. In 1939 the NAAFI ran 600 canteens and had 4,000 personnel in total, with the British Expeditionary Force, based in northern France in 1939 and 1940, supported by 230 canteens and 2,300 NAAFI staff. By 1944 the organisation had expanded massively, being responsible for 7,000 canteens and 96,000 personnel, in barracks, shore establishments, airbases and on board ships the world over. Many staff were recruited from among grocers and shopkeepers to man the expanding service.[1]

The NAAFI provided servicemen with the opportunity to supplement their meagre rations and to alleviate what could at times be a grim existence. The NAAFI is known, for good reason, as 'the service to the services', and aside from the stereotypical image of tea and cakes, the NAAFI also provided other comforts such as clothing, toiletries, stationery, newspapers and books.[2] In austere times such seemingly insignificant comforts could do wonders for morale.

The most hazardous role for NAAFI personnel came on board warships. With the Royal Navy's reserve fleet being re-activated, new ships being built and merchant vessels being converted into warships, there was a chronic demand for NAAFI personnel to provide each warship with a canteen. In 1939 the NAAFI ran 266 canteens on board Royal Navy ships; by the end of 1945 this figure had grown to 1,590.[3] Most canteens were run by a manager, who was assisted by a number of canteen assitants, depending on the size of the ship and the crew that they had to serve.

Whilst at sea the NAAFI employees faced exactly the same dangers as the other members of the ship's company. This was shown in the Falklands War in 1982, when John Leake, the

The grave of Canteen Manager
George Huggins in Kingston
Cemetery. The personal message on
his gravestone confirms that he died
of wounds received when his ship was
attacked. *(Author)*

NAAFI canteen manager on board HMS *Ardent*, himself an ex-soldier, became frustrated with sheltering from air attack and went up on deck to man an anti-aircraft machine gun and was later decorated.[4] At action stations NAAFI personnel usually assisted in moving ammunition up to the guns.[5] And sadly, when a ship was sunk, NAAFI employees were at exactly the same risk as the other crew members – at sea there is no option of going to the rear, out of harm's way. Wherever a ship went, so went the men on board her.

Running a NAAFI canteen on board a warship could be a challenging task indeed; for example, canteen managers were often not told when a ship was due to leave port until shortly before its departure for security reasons. Other problems included keeping adequate stores on board a ship, in particular smaller vessels, especially if she was to remain at sea for a long period of time; shipping goods to far-flung stations or ships at sea, with a shortage of stores ships to transport the goods; and procuring enough goods to sell, with Britain under blockade by U-boats for much of the early part of the war.[6]

The NAAFI's first losses came within weeks of war being declared. Canteen Assistant Harold Matheson was on board the aircraft carrier HMS *Courageous* when she was torpedoed by *U-29* on 19 September 1939, literally days after the start of the war. Originally a cruiser, the *Courageous* had been converted to an aircraft carrier in the mid-1920s, and was on an anti-submarine patrol off the coast of Ireland when she was lost.[7] As well as Matheson, the canteen manager and three other canteen assistants were lost.[8]

Kingston Cemetery, the last resting place for many Portsmouth servicemen of the Second World War. *(Author)*

The Royal Navy, and Portsmouth, suffered another major loss less than a month later. Canteen Assistant Alan Daysh, 19 and from Cosham, was on board the battleship HMS *Royal Oak* when she was sunk in Scapa Flow on 14 October 1939. Also on board the *Royal Oak* was Canteen Assistant Harold White. Appropriately enough, a NAAFI launch was amongst the first boats on the scene searching for survivors. The loss of the *Courageous* and the *Royal Oak* so early in the war is evidence that there was no 'phoney war' at sea, nor for the NAAFI. Daysh and White were not the only NAAFI personnel from Portsmouth to be lost on battleships, however, as on 24 May 1941 Canteen Assistant Frank Ayling was on board the battlecruiser HMS *Hood* when she was sunk by the *Bismarck*. In total, seven NAAFI personnel were lost on the *Hood*.[9] This shows not only their sacrifice, but also how few staff there were to serve a ship with a crew of over a thousand men.

NAAFI personnel were also at risk while at sea in coastal waters. Canteen Manager Gordon Huggins, 36 and from North End, was serving on HMS *Foylebank*, which was a 5,500-ton merchant vessel that had been requisitioned and pressed into service with the Royal Navy as an anti-aircraft ship. On 4 July 1940 she was moored in Portland Harbour, and most of the crew were at breakfast when unidentified aircraft were spotted. They turned out to be twenty-six Stuka divebombers, sent specifically to attack the *Foylebank*. Twenty-two bombs hit the ship, causing raging fires and cutting all the power. She sank the next day, and out of a crew of 300 men, 176 were killed and only forty survivors escaped injury.[10] Gordon Huggins died four days later and is buried in Kingston Cemetery.

Canteen Manager Alfred West, from Copnor, was serving on board the cruiser HMS *Southampton*. The *Southampton* was taking part in an operation escorting convoys to Malta when she was attacked by twelve Stukas. The cruiser was hit by at least two bombs and a blaze spread from the bow to the stern, killing eighty-one men. Without power and seriously damaged, she was torpedoed by HMS *Gloucester* and HMS *Orion* after the remaining crew had abandoned ship.

The Mediterranean saw heavy losses for the Royal Navy, and also the NAAFI by default. Canteen Assistant James Henwood, 19 and from Southsea, was on board HMS *Kashmir* when he was killed on 23 May 1941. Built not far from Portsmouth at Woolston in Southampton, the *Kashmir* was sunk south of Crete by Stuka divebombers. Canteen Assistant Leslie Ayling, 20, was on board HMS *Calcutta* when he was killed on 1 June 1941. An anti-aircraft cruiser, the *Calcutta* was sunk by Junkers 88 divebombers off Alexandria, with the loss of nineteen of her crew.

One NAAFI canteen assistant from Portsmouth was lost much further afield. Lionel Matthews, 22 and from North End, was on board HMS *Dunedin* when she was sunk by *U-124* on 24 November 1941. The *Dunedin* had been operating in the Carribean and the central Atlantic when she was torpedoed north-east of Brazil. Only four officers and sixty-three men survived from her crew of 486. Twenty-six of those lost came from Portsmouth.

Meanwhile, the losses continued in the Mediterranean as Canteen Manager James Noyce, 34 and from North End, was killed on board HMS *Galatea* when it was torpedoed by *U-557* off Alexandria on 15 December 1941. Canteen Manager Leonard Sly, 23 and from Mile End, was serving on board the light cruiser HMS *Neptune* when she was sunk in the Mediterranean on 19 December 1941. Built in Portsmouth Dockyard in the early 1930s, HMS *Neptune* was lost after hitting a minefield off Tripoli, Libya. Ironically, Lieutenant Commander William Hussey, a Portsmouth officer, had attempted to take his ship HMS *Lively* into the minefield to tow HMS *Neptune* out, but was forced back.[11]

Canteen Manager Edgar New, 24, was on board HMS *Audacity* when he died on 22 December 1941. Originally a German merchant ship, *Audacity* was captured in 1940 and converted into an escort aircraft carrier. Whilst escorting a convoy from Gibraltar to Britain, the *Audacity* was torpedoed by *U-751*, 500 miles west of Brittany.

Canteen Manager Henry Aldridge, from Copnor, was killed on 4 March 1942 when HMS *Anking* was sunk. The *Anking* was a depot ship hired by the Royal Navy, and was torpedoed by the Japanese off Java, Indonesia. Thus Henry Aldridge was the only Portsmouth NAAFI employee to be killed by the Japanese.

For the first few years of the war NAAFI personnel served as civilians but came under military discipline when afloat. This naturally proved confusing when personnel were at sea, as although they generally performed as part of the crew, civilians serving alongside enlisted men proved to be an anomaly. In August 1942, however, the Royal Navy Canteen Service was formed, and NAAFI staff on board ships were fully enrolled into the Royal Navy for the duration of the war. Bringing NAAFI personnel under military discipline gave canteen staff protection as servicemen if they were ever captured, as on a number of occasions the Germans had treated captured civilians as spies or saboteurs.[12]

Two NAAFI personnel from Portsmouth were lost after becoming part of the Royal Navy. Canteen Manager Frederick Coles, 33 and from Copnor, was killed when HMS *Hursley* was lost on 2 September 1943, and is remembered on the Chatham Naval Memorial. Canteen Manager Ernest Jago, 28 and from Milton, was serving at the HMS *Victory* shore establishment in Portsmouth when he died on 24 February 1945, and is buried in Milton Cemetery.

It is noticeable that no NAAFI personnel from Portsmouth were killed whilst serving either the army or the Royal Air Force. Ships of the Royal Navy were at risk of attack as soon as they left port, while NAAFI canteens and other support services were usually kept well to the rear on land. The RAF's NAAFI canteens were also relatively safe on air bases, although they were at risk of attack during the early years of the war, particularly during the Battle of Britain and the Blitz.

It is also striking that most of Portsmouth's NAAFI casualties came during the first few years of the war, when British ships were being sunk at a significant rate. These losses also show not only how often the Royal Navy was routinely under threat from German divebombers, U-boats and mines, but also how the NAAFI staff faced exactly the same risk as the men they were serving. A total of 258 NAAFI staff were lost whilst serving the Royal Navy.[13]

To this day the NAAFI is still a central part of the armed forces, and has been the source of sustenance and relief for millions of British servicemen and women.

17

Women at War

WOMEN WERE MORE involved in working towards victory during the Second World War than in any previous conflict. Given the shortage of manpower, women were increasingly given more and more tasks to perform that would have been unthinkable during peacetime. And as a naval town, the women of Portsmouth knew all too well about the demands of serving in the armed forces and the horrors of war.

The government was initially reluctant to conscript women, but the demands of total war left little option. In December 1941 the National Service Act called up unmarried women between 20 and 30 to join one of the auxiliary services, while married women were called up later. By mid-1943, 90 per cent of single women and 80 per cent of married women were in some kind of work.[1] Women mostly joined three services: the Women's Royal Naval Services (WRNS or Wrens), the Auxiliary Territorial Service (ATS) and the Women's Auxiliary Air Force (WAAF). A smaller number also served in organisations such as the Red Cross.

Sixteen women from Portsmouth are known to have died whilst serving in the armed forces or other uniformed services during the Second World War. The recollections of many of their fellow servicewomen have been recorded for posterity and give us a valuable impression of not only how important their work was, but also how the war changed women's role in society forever.

The Women's Royal Navy Service was originally formed during the First World War and was revived on the outbreak of war in 1939. The recruiting slogan, 'Join the Wrens – free a man for the fleet', described the service's role succinctly – every support job filled by a woman enabled a male sailor to serve in a more active role.

At its peak in 1944 the WRNS had over 75,000 members, and over 102 Wrens died during the war, while twenty-two were wounded.[2] Eight Portsmouth Wrens were killed. Not surprisingly, joining the Wrens was a natural choice for many women from Portsmouth, as many of them had fathers, brothers and husbands in the Royal Navy. For Kay Childs, who was born in Outram Road, Southsea, in 1920, the choice of which service to join was a straightforward one:

Wrens on parade at HMS *Vernon*. *(Portsmouth Museums and Records Service)*

Obviously I was going to join one of the forces and there'd never been any question in my mind which one. I suppose being in a naval city that ... I had a brother who was already a Royal Marine. Oh, I don't think it would have entered my head to join any of the other ...[3]

Wren Gladys Cooper, from Hilsea, was based at HMS *Excellent* on Whale Island when she died on 19 November 1941, and is buried in Milton Cemetery. Leading Wren Kathleen Bennett, 22 and from Copnor, died on 5 July 1944 and is buried in Milton Cemetery. Wren Joyce Chapman, 22 and from Eastney, was based at HMS *Victory*, the Royal Naval barracks in Portsmouth, when she died on 12 January 1945 and is buried in Milton Cemetery. Wren Ethel Field, 22 and from Portsmouth, was based at HMS *Excellent* when she died on 22 August 1945 and is buried in Milton Cemetery. Leading Wren Peggy Bennett, 24 and from Southsea, died on 1 September 1945 and is buried in Milton Cemetery. Leading Wren Dorothy Harris, 36 and from Buckland, was based at HMS *Victory* when she died on 12 February 1946, and is buried in Kingston Cemetery. Wren Peggy Carter, 23 and from Stamshaw, died on 21 October 1946 and is buried in Milton Cemetery. Lastly, Wren Marjorie Bayliss, 36, was based at HMS *Excellent* when she died on 22 July 1947, and is buried at South Baddesley, Lymington.

It is striking how five of the eight Portsmouth Wrens to die during the period marked by the Commonwealth War Graves Commission actually died after the end of the war in Europe. This suggests not only that more women joined the services later in the war, but also that women remained in uniform for some time after the end of hostilities. All of the Wrens from Portsmouth were serving in Portsmouth, suggesting that there was a huge demand for women to work at the shore establishments in the area.

Women were no longer a wartime-only presence in the Royal Navy as the Women's Royal Naval Service remained after the war – recognition, if any were needed, of the vital role that women had played. The Wrens, however, were not fully integrated with the rest of the Royal Navy until 1993.

The Auxiliary Territorial Service was formed on 9 September 1938, during the British army's hurried preparations for war after the Munich Crisis. The first recruits were cooks, clerks and storekeepers, and women aged between 17 and 43 were allowed to join. This meant that girls who were too young for the Wrens could join the ATS instead.

The ATS reached 65,000 members by 1941, and ATS girls were given increasingly specialised and important jobs, such as orderlies, drivers, postal workers and ammunition inspectors. Hessie Hare explained the range of jobs open to women, and how she came to be an officers' mess steward:

Yes, there were several choices for office work and things like that but I'd never done any office work so it was useless really to do it but I quite enjoyed what I did anyway ... I was a waitress or steward, I suppose they call them now, I worked in the officers' mess, cleaning it, waiting at tables, washing up all sorts of things, pressing trousers if they needed them done.[4]

Women were barred from serving in battle, but due to growing shortages of men ATS girls took over more and more active functions, including manning anti-aircraft guns and searchlights. By VE Day there were 190,000 members of the ATS, and it is believed that a total of 172 ATS girls were killed during the war.[5]

The ATS seems to have been less scrupulous about its recruiting, taking younger girls and requiring less identification than the Wrens for example. Hessie Hare attempted to join the Wrens, but found that she had to be 18. The ATS, on the other hand, allowed her to join at the age of 17. This policy contrasts starkly with the situation for young men, who had to wait until the age of 18 to join the army but could join the Royal Navy much younger, as young as 14 for boy seamen.

Five women from Portsmouth were killed serving with the ATS during the Second World War. Volunteer Mabel Scott was 18 and from Copnor when she died on 24 August 1940, and is buried in Christ Church Cemetery, Portsdown. She was the daughter of John and Charlotte Scott, and died early in the war before women were given the same ranks as men. It is thought that Mabel Scott was killed in one of the first major air raids on Portsmouth, when sixty-seven bombs were dropped by forty-seven aircraft, killing 125 people.[6]

Private Evelyn Spittles, 24 and from Fratton, died on 18 March 1942 and is buried in Milton Cemetery. She was the daughter of Mr and Mrs Francis Spittles. Private Enid Lucie, from North End, died on 24 June 1943 and is buried in Kingston Cemetery. She was the daughter of William and Amy Lucie. Private Winifred Lewis, 21 and from Cosham, was attached to the Royal Artillery when she died on 7 August 1943, and buried in St Peter and St Paul's churchyard, Wymering. She was the daughter of Charles and Millie Lewis. Private Audrey Leppard, 18 and from Fratton, was attached to 591st Battery, 183rd (M) Heavy Anti-aircraft Regiment of the Royal Artillery when she died on 28 October 1943, and is buried in Kingston Cemetery. She was the daughter of William and Margaret Leppard.

The grave of Private Audrey Leppard, an 18-year-old ATS girl attached to the Royal Artillery, in Kingston Cemetery. *(Author)*

Nancy Jackson served as a shorthand typist with the ATS and had a positive experience:

I thoroughly enjoyed it. I enjoyed meeting people from all walks of life, I enjoyed the company. I enjoyed the drill, the Army life, everything to do with it I thoroughly enjoyed. I made a lot of friends.[7]

Originally, ATS companies were formed to support the RAF, but it was eventually found that a dedicated organisation was needed. The Women's Auxiliary Air Force was created on 28 July 1939.[8] Membership of the WAAF was initially voluntary, before the conscription of women began in 1941. Up until then women were allowed to leave the service any time they liked, but after 1941 WAAFs came under military discipline, and either joined for four years or for the duration of the war.[9] Women did not serve as aircrew on the front line, but were involved in duties such as parachute packing, manning barrage balloons, providing catering, working as radar operators, driving, communications, working on codebreaking and intelligence, and as plotters in operations rooms. Some women with flying experience also ferried aircraft from factories to airbases. The demands of wartime and a shortage of men meant that women took on more skilled and technical jobs than ever before, breaking down traditional boundaries in the workplace.[10]

ATS girls manning a 3.7in anti-aircraft gun site near Portsmouth. (The News)

Two aircraftwomen from Portsmouth died during the war. The first was Aircraftwoman Second Class Violet Sampson, 31 and from Southsea, who died on 9 April 1942 and is buried in Highland Road Cemetery. Her service number suggests that she joined the WAAF after May 1941. Aircraftwoman Second Class Joyce Botting, 22 and from East Cosham, died on 3 April 1944 and is buried in Westbourne, near Portsmouth. Her service number suggests that she joined the WAAF after January 1943. Other voluntary services also played a vital role in the war effort, with both the British Red Cross and St John Ambulance providing first aid, particularly when the emergency services were hard pressed during bomb raids. Nurse Rita Harfield, 23 and from Southsea, died whilst serving with a Red Cross Voluntary Aid Detachment on 18 May 1944. She is buried in Kingston Cemetery.

Most women seem to have enjoyed their war service, unless perhaps they had been unfortunate enough to serve under an unpleasant NCO or officer. Many accounts from servicewomen recall the companionship that they felt with their colleagues:

We had some fun. No, we were quite friendly all of us. We all lived in the one room in the college, so we all got to know each other very well … it was quite fun really.[11]

Overall the experiences of women during the war seem to have been positive. Young women who might never have left Portsmouth were given the opportunity to travel more widely, meet other young people from around Britain and beyond, and learn new skills and responsibilities that might have been unthinkable in pre-war society. Many women learnt to drive and it became far more common for women to wear trousers. A woman's role in the workplace also changed, as remembered by Kay Childs:

> You see the role of women has changed enormously since the war. Before the war it wasn't at all unusual that I left school and there was no question of having a job. That wouldn't be so now. [12]

Many aspects of service life were markedly unequal for women, however. In the WAAF, for example, women only received two-thirds of the pay of their male equivalents and were only allocated four-fifths of their daily rations. [13] Also, although the war had broken down some boundaries, there could still be some resentment, particularly at the way in which women had performed technical and skilled jobs that were traditionally a male preserve.

Servicewomen from Portsmouth had been at the forefront of one of the biggest social changes brought about by the Second World War, and Nancy Jackson felt that the war had changed women's role in society virtually overnight:

> It had a completely lasting effect. My entire life changed from what it had been as a child. [14]

18

The Merchant Navy

AS AN ISLAND nation, merchant shipping had long been vital for sustaining Britain, and the British Empire itself was largely built on seaborne commercial trade. This trade gave rise to a large fleet of merchant vessels, and a powerful Royal Navy to protect them and the seas that they sailed. During the Second World War the British Merchant Navy bore a serious burden and suffered grievous losses keeping Britain's lifeline to the colonies alive and maintaining supply lines with theatres of war in areas such as North Africa and the Far East. One historian has accurately described seaborne trade during the war as Britain's 'maritime jugular', demonstrating both its importance and also its vulnerability.[1]

In 1939 the British Merchant Navy was the largest in the world. However, most merchant vessels were old, and the fleet had suffered from a lack of investment during the depression of the 1930s.[2] Merchant seamen were a varied band of men: from the very young to the very old, those running from the law or other problems, and also a sizeable contingent of foreign seamen, known as 'Lascars'.

During the war the Merchant Navy and merchant seamen themselves came under the Ministry of Shipping, and ultimately the authority of the Admiralty. Despite this, the conditions and terms of service were poor, and their pay stopped the moment their ship was sunk, meaning that survivors of sunken merchantmen could ponder not only their chances of survival, but also their unemployment as they sat in their lifeboat. In addition, unlike their Royal Navy counterparts, they could not expect survivor's leave.[3]

A total of 11.7 million tons of British shipping was sunk between 1939 and 1945, which amounted to some 54 per cent of the size of the Merchant Navy at the start of the war, and 2,426 British vessels are believed to have been lost, with losses peaking at around twenty ships a week during May 1941.[4] Around 30,248 merchant seamen were killed in action during the war and forty-two of them are known to have come from Portsmouth.[5] However, despite their huge sacrifice, the men of the Merchant Navy received little recognition during or after the war.

The grave of Engineer Officer Albert Lofting, killed on the SS *Irishman*, in Kingston cemetery in Portsmouth. *(Author)*

One of Portsmouth's first Merchant Navy losses came on 10 July 1940, when the SS *British Chancellor*, a 7,000-ton tanker, was berthed at Falmouth and came under air attack by the Luftwaffe.[6] Second Engineer William Crocker, aged 36, was killed and is buried in Falmouth.

On 8 May 1941 another loss was experienced in local waters when the 99-ton tug SS *Irishman* hit a mine in Langstone Harbour and sank. On board were Engineer Officer Albert Lofting, aged 58, and Ordinary Seaman Colin Duke, aged just 16. Lofting is buried in Kingston Cemetery and Duke is remembered on the Tower Hill Memorial in London. The wreck of the *Irishman* was still intact in shallow water until the 1990s, when it was blown up as a shipping hazard.[7]

The biggest loss of Portsmouth merchant seamen in one incident came on 20 September 1941. Given the manner in which the Merchant Navy operated all around the world, it is perhaps sadly ironic that the biggest single losses in one incident were experienced in the Solent, when the Isle of Wight paddle steamer ferry SS *Portsdown* was sunk by a mine.

Operated by Southern Railways, the *Portsdown* had taken part in the Dunkirk evacuation earlier in the war and received damage taking troops off the beaches. She had also made a number of voyages between Portsmouth and Southampton on war service during 1940 and 1941.[8] In order to give her crew protection in the event of air attack her wheelhouse was surrounded with concrete blocks.

On 20 September 1941 the *Portsdown* was making the early morning mail run to the island when she passed through the Swashway Channel, near Spitbank Fort. The ship was full of servicemen travelling to and from the Isle of Wight. Among them was Ann Lupton, a member of the Women's Auxiliary Air Force, returning to the Isle of Wight after a wireless course:

> I got on to the boat … I was the only WAAF there and they put me into a first class compartment and gave me a cup of tea and said 'stop there' because the rest of the boat is full with troops going over to the island and that.[9]

The *Portsdown* left Portsmouth Harbour Station at 3 a.m., and some sources put the number of passengers at around sixty – it is likely that the true number will never be known as the authorities did not keep details of passengers.[10] In fact, after the disaster, local army authorities expressed concern at the manner in which the Isle of Wight ferries were being managed, with no officer or NCO in charge of the servicemen and no records of exactly who was on board.[11]

As she was passing through the Swashway the *Portsdown* hit a mine. The ship broke in two; the forward section sank and the stern came to rest on a sandbank. Ann Lupton had gone outside to get some fresh air when the explosion occurred:

> … we were standing there talking and all of a sudden there was this big explosion and I remember getting hit, even to this day, getting hit on the side of my nose and falling to the floor … I thought I was going to die. I honestly did and when, when we sort of struggled to our feet and you expected to be drowned, you expected the water to come in, because of the suction noise and you could hear the groaning of the steam boat or what not, or the timbers and, it was really horrible and I can still remember it to this day.[12]

The SS *Portsdown* photographed before the war. *(Ian Boyle of Simplon Postcards)*

Along with the other female survivors, Ann Lupton was put into a lifeboat. One of the soldiers had even managed to pick up a bottle of spirits from the saloon bar before leaving the *Portsdown*; the bottle was passed around and incredibly Ann Lupton was even given a glass to drink out of.

A rescue operation sprang to work immediately. Searchlights from Portsmouth's coastal defences were shone on the area, and small naval boats were sent out to rescue survivors, with many of the wounded being taken to Haslar Hospital. By 6 a.m., when the Southern Railways marine manager arrived on the scene, there were no more survivors or bodies to be found, although some of the mailbags were later retrieved. Minesweepers were sent to ensure that any other mines were cleared.

Twenty-nine servicemen are believed to have been on board the *Portsdown* – twelve were killed. Only three of the crew survived, with seven of those killed from Portsmouth: the purser Edward Cottrell, 34 and from Southsea; Deck Hand Alfred Farey, 61 and from Fratton; Fireman William Harrison, 47 and from North End; Fireman Bertram Rawlins, 25 and from Buckland; Deck Hand John Monk, 27 and from Southsea; Ordinary Seaman Edwin Burnett, 19 and from Eastney; and Mate Seth Burgess, 33 and from Southsea. Burgess' body was recovered and he is buried in Milton Cemetery, while the rest of the crew were lost at sea and are remembered on the Tower Hill Memorial. A memorial service was later held at Portsmouth cathedral. For some of the survivors the scars lasted for many years. Ann Lupton had been struck on the face by a pipe and still had oil in the side of her face twenty years later.

Modern Isle of Wight ferries sail through the Swashway Channel, almost exactly over the site of the sinking of the *Portsdown*. *(Author)*

The grave of Seth Burgess, mate on the SS *Portsdown*, in Milton Cemetery in Portsmouth. *(Author)*

Extremely heavy losses were endured by the Merchant Navy during the Battle of the Atlantic, in particular during 1941, 1942 and 1943, when the U-boat wolf packs operated in the North Atlantic and elsewhere. The Germans were well aware of the importance of Britain's dependence on imports from abroad: if the U-boats could cut the umbilical cord, perhaps Britain might be brought to her knees.

The first Portsmouth merchant seaman to be sunk by a U-boat was Cadet Robert Tickell, 20, who was a crew member of the MV *Zealandic*. Weighing in at 10,000 tons, she was just starting a long voyage from Liverpool to Australia via Panama when she was torpedoed on 17 January 1941 by *U-106*, north-west of Rockall in the Atlantic. Seventy-three men were killed, with no survivors. Tickell is remembered on the Tower Hill Memorial.

Losses began to mount from early 1941, and on 16 February 1941 Third Officer Campbell Morrison, 24, was lost on SS *Gairsoppa*. A 5,000-ton steamer built in 1919, the *Gairsoppa* was sunk by *U-101* 300 miles south of Ireland, while sailing from Calcutta to Liverpool. Eighty-four men were killed and there was only one survivor. The next day, Fourth Engineering Officer Percival Rogers, 27 and from Cosham, was lost on MV *Siamese Prince*. The 8,000-ton *Siamese Prince* was sailing between New York and Liverpool when she was sunk south-west of the Faroe Islands by *U-69*. Fifty-seven men were killed and there were no survivors.

Chief Engine Room Officer Stanley Freshwater, 36 and from North End, was lost when the SS *Petrel* was sunk on 26 September 1941. A small 1,000-ton ship, the *Petrel* was sailing

The Tower Hill
Memorial in London.
Nearly 32,000 merchant
seamen lost at sea during
the Second World War
are commemorated on
the memorial. *(Flickr user
Iain McLauchlan)*

from Porto to Bristol when she was sunk by *U-124* north of the Azores. Twenty-two men were killed, but nine survived.

In late 1942 several troopships were lost with Portsmouth sailors on board. Second Radio Officer Walter Vince, 42 and from Southsea, was lost when the 11,000-ton MV *Abosso*, en route from Cape Town to Liverpool, was torpedoed by *U-575* in the North Atlantic. Three hundred and sixty-two men were killed and there were only thirty-one survivors. On 14 November two troopships were sunk: the 16,000-ton P&O ship SS *Narkunda* was lost in an air raid en route between North Africa and England. Thirty-one men were killed; among them was Boilermaker Reginald Brading, aged 44. Also lost on the same day was William Gibson, 42 and from Southsea. Gibson was the barkeeper on board MV *Warwick Castle*, a 20,000-ton troopship sunk by *U-413* between Gibraltar and Glasgow, 200 miles off Portugal. Ninety-six men were killed, but 366 survivors were rescued.

The U-boats ventured out much further than the North Atlantic in an effort to cut Britain's maritime lifeline further afield. On 13 October 1942 the SS *Empire Nomad*, a brand-new 7,000-ton steamer, was sunk 250 miles south of Cape Town by *U-159*. Among the ten men killed was Second Radio Officer Ernest Fuller, 27 and from Cosham.

Few Merchant Navy losses were experienced from late 1943 onwards, although there were still casualties. The Allies had managed to crack the German navy's Enigma codes, giving them vital information about U-boat movements. Anti-submarine defences were also perfected, such as sonar and the pom-pom anti-submarine weapon.[13] With such improvements in technology and weaponry, the closing of the 'mid-Atlantic gap' and improved escort vessels, such as the Flower-class Corvette, British and Allied merchantmen could sail the seas with increased, but not complete, safety.

The sea could still be a dangerous place in wartime, however. The hospital ship SS *Amsterdam* hit a mine off Juno beach in Normandy on 7 August 1944 whilst evacuating the wounded. Fifty-five wounded men, ten medical staff, thirty crew members and eleven German prisoners of war were killed. One of the crewmen lost was Fireman Ronald Copping, 18 and from Fratton, and he is remembered on the Tower Hill Memorial.

Although most merchant shipping was sunk by enemy U-boats and a few by air attack, one Portsmouth seaman was killed when German E-boats, the equivalent of the British motor torpedo boats, attacked his ship on 31 January 1944. Robert Baird, 56 and from Southsea, was the third engineering officer on board SS *Caleb Sprague*, which was a small coaster vessel that had only been built in 1943. She was sailing between London and Newport, South Wales, when she was attacked by E-boats off Beachy Head. Twenty-two crew members were killed and only five survived. The loss of the *Caleb Sprague* demonstrates how small coastal vessels were used to move supplies around Britain, and also how the English Channel was not necessarily safe even in January 1944, less than five months before the D-Day landings.

Most Merchant Navy losses came in the North Atlantic, Mediterranean or the English Channel, but one Portsmouth man was killed serving in the Indian Ocean. Able Seaman Leonard Morris, aged 26, was serving on board the SS *British Chivalry* when she was torpedoed by a Japanese submarine on 23 February 1944. A 7,000-ton tanker, the *British Chivalry* went down in the middle of the Indian Ocean, and it was reported that survivors were machine-gunned. Miraculously, thirty-eight survivors were later rescued after thirty-seven days in life rafts. Morris is remembered on the Tower Hill Memorial.

The Tower Hill Memorial in London remembers the sacrifice of the thousands of merchant seamen of Britain and her colonies, in both world wars. On the north bank of the Thames, near the Tower of London, the names of seafarers who have no known grave are remembered. Fittingly the memorial is close to London's Docklands, which had played such an important role in the growth of the British Empire hundreds of years before.

Although history has naturally lavished much attention on the forces that are seen as having won the war, that the Merchant Navy ensured that Britain did not lose the war should never be forgotten, neither should the sacrifices of its unsung heroes. It is also important to recognise the role that the Merchant Navy played in supporting the other armed forces, by transporting equipment, weapons, supplies and troops to and from the theatres of war, often at great peril.

Notes

1 *'Duty nobly done': Chief Petty Officer Reginald Ellingworth GC*

1   TNA ADM 188/699: Service Record of Reginald Ellingworth.
2   GRO Lancashire 8e p. 2454, September Quarter 1919.
3   GRO Lancashire 8e p. 1150, March Quarter 1925.
4   GRO Portsmouth 2b p. 906, March Quarter 1925.
5   PCL Electoral Registers; *Kelly's* (1940); GRO Romford 4a 944B, December Quarter 1940.
6   TNA HO 186/1518: Unexploded parachute mines: reports and disposal.
7   Owen, James, *Danger UXB: The Heroic Story of the WWII Bomb Disposal Teams* (London, Little, Brown, 2010), p. 163.
8   Owen, *Danger UXB*, p. 165.
9   Lockwood, Martyn, 'The End of the Phoney War' (Essex Police Museum History Notebook, No 26).
10 TNA HO 186/1518.
11 TNA HO 198/231: Record of parachute mines dropped by enemy aircraft.
12 TNA PREM 3/314/2: Prime Minister's correspondence papers.
13 TNA PREM 3/314/2.
14 TNA PREM 3/314/2.
15 TNA PREM 3/341/2.
16 Millar, John, *A Portrait of a Family* (privately published), p. 269. I am grateful to Trevor Ellingworth for providing this reference.
17 Cashford MBE, RNVR, *Noel, Bang! Stories of Bangs from 1917 to the Present Day* (Sheffield, ALD Print, 2008), p. 17.
18 Turner, John Frayn, *Awards of the George Cross 1940–2005* (Barnsley, Pen and Sword, 2010), pp. 16–8.
19 Millar, *A Portrait of a Family*, p. 269.
20 Millar, *A Portrait of a Family*, p. 264.
21 Millar, *A Portrait of a Family*, p. 272. Commander Moore was also awarded the George Cross.
22 TNA HO 186/636. Between September 1940 and June 1941 twenty-nine mines were dropped on Dagenham, and twenty-nine on Barking.
23 BDL: letter from Mr J. Millar (30 April 1997).
24 BDL: letter from Mr A.W. Snow (22 March 1993).

25 BDL: letter from Mr J. Millar (12 September 1997).

26 Millar, *A Portrait of a Family*, p. 265.

27 Millar, *A Portrait of a Family*, p. 266.

28 TNA HO 186/1518.

29 TNA HO 186/1518.

30 *EN* (24 September 1940).

31 *EN* (4 October 1940).

32 Owen, *Danger UXB*, p. 165.

33 *LG* (17 December 1940).

34 *EN* (21 December 1940).

35 TNA PREM 3/314/2.

36 *The Times* (24 April 1997).

37 Ellingworth's George Cross is now on display in the Imperial War Museum's new Ashcroft Gallery of Victoria and George Crosses, which opened in 2010.

38 Millar, *A Portrait of a Family*, p. 271.

39 *BDR* (24 September 1998).

40 *BDR* (13 May 1999).

2 *The Battleships: HMS* Royal Oak, *HMS* Hood *and HMS* Barham

1 Whitmarsh, Andrew, *Portsmouth at War* (Stroud, Tempus, 2007), p. 91.

2 Snyder, Gerald S., *The Royal Oak Disaster* (William Kimber, 1976), p. 73.

3 TNA ADM 188/834: Frederick Bealing service record.

4 PMRS Doris Bealing OHI 2331A.

5 McKee, Alexander, *Black Saturday: The Tragedy of the Royal Oak* (Souvenir Press, 1959), p. 41.

6 McKee, *Black Saturday*, p. 14.

7 Snyder, *Royal Oak*, p. 113.

8 McKee, *Black Saturday*, p. 16.

9 McKee, *Black Saturday*, p. 79.

10 McKee, *Black Saturday*, p. 85.

11 Turner, D., *Last Dawn: The Royal Oak Tragedy at Scapa Flow* (Glendaruel, Argyll publishing, 2009), p. 53.

12 McKee, *Black Saturday*, p. 138.

13 McKee, *Black Saturday*, p. 73.

14 McKee, *Black Saturday*, p. 134.

15 A shore base, renamed HMS *Nelson* soon after the end of the war.

16 PMRS Bealing OHI 2331A.

17 *EN* (16 October 1939).

18 PMRS Iris Harris OHI 5426A-1.

19 Hoyt, Edwin P., *The Life and Death of HMS Hood* (Littlehampton Book Services, 1977), p. 38.

20 Bradford, Ernle, *The Mighty Hood* (The Book Service, 1974), p. 103.

21 Hoyt, *Life and Death*, p. 109.

22 Hoyt, *Life and Death*, p. 41.

23 Bradford, *Mighty Hood*, pp. 54, 140.

24 Norman, Andrew, *HMS Hood: Pride of the Royal Navy* (Gloucestershire, Spellmount, 2002), p. 90.

25 Norman, *Pride of the Royal Navy*, p. 57.

26 Norman, *Pride of the Royal Navy*, p. 80.

27 Bradford, *Mighty Hood*, p. 206.

28 Hoyt, *Life and Death*, p. 137.

29 Bradford, *Mighty Hood*, p. 186.

30 PMRS Leslie Matthews OHI 5385A.

31 Jones, Geoffrey, *Battleship Barham* (William Kimber, 1979), p. 40.

32 Jones, *Barham*, p. 11.

33   Cunningham, Admiral Sir A.N., *A Sailor's Odyssey* (London, Hutchinson, 1952).

34   Correspondence with Chris Eldridge, Ray and Doug Green's nephew.

35   Stevenson, Jason, 'The Barham Conspiracy', *World War II Magazine*, December 2004. Interestingly, for security reasons during the war sailors did not wear the name of their ship on their cap tally, only 'HMS'.

36   Stevenson, 'Barham Conspiracy'.

3 *Portsmouth's Boy Sailors*

1   According to research by the author, at least nineteen underage boys are known to have been killed serving with the British army in the First World War. The true figure is likely to be higher.

2   Private Bobby Johns, killed serving with the Parachute Regiment in Normandy. He was 16.

3   Phillipson, David, *Band of Brothers: Boy Seamen in the Royal Navy, 1800–1956* (Stroud, Sutton, 1996), p. 101.

4   Sugden, John, *Nelson: A Dream of Glory* (London, Jonathan Cape, 2004), p. 47.

5   Phillipson, *Band of Brothers*, p. 1.

6   TNA ADM 188/699: Reginald Ellingworth service record; ADM 188/757: Henry Miller service record.

7   *LG* (16 August 1940 and 17 December 1940).

8   TNA ADM 196/150: William Hussey service record.

9   Wragg, David, *Royal Navy Handbook 1939–1945* (Stroud, Sutton, 2006), p. 124.

10   Phillipson, *Band of Brothers*, p. 37.

11   Snyder, Gerald S., *The Royal Oak Disaster* (William Kimber, 1976), p. 104.

12   Norman, Andrew, *HMS Hood: Pride of the Royal Navy* (Stroud, Spellmount, 2009), p. 25.

13   McKee, Alexander, *Black Saturday: The Tragedy of the Royal Oak* (Souvenir Press, 1959), p. 73.

14   Hansard: HC Debate, Boys (Active Service) 25 October 1939 vol. 352 cc1400–1; Dr Edith Summerskill MP and Reginald Sorensen MP to Winston Churchill MP.

15   TNA ADM 178/123: Employment of boys on seagoing ships.

16   TNA ADM 178/123.

17   www.navalhistory.net.

18   Hansard House of Commons Debate, Navy Estimates 11 March 1937 vol. 321 cc1367–508; Kenneth Lindsay MP (Civil Lord to the Admiralty).

19   www.navalhistory.net.

20   Wragg, *Royal Navy Handbook*, p. 124.

4 *'Most promising, should go far': Lieutenant Commander William Hussey DSO, DSC*

1   TNA ADM 196/150/228: Service record of William Hussey. Unless otherwise noted all subsequent details regarding Hussey's career are either taken from his service record or the relevant edition of the *Navy List*.

2   Pridham-Wippell rose to become a vice-admiral and second-in-command of the Mediterranean fleet during the Second World War. He survived the sinking of his flagship, HMS *Barham*.

3   GRO: Marylebone 1a 1575, September Quarter 1933.

4   *NL* (November 1933).

5   *NL* (October 1934).

6   *NL* (December 1935).

7   *NL* (March 1936).

8   *NL* (December 1937).

9   *LG* (23 December 1939). Unfortunately there are no details to elaborate on the actions for which Hussey was awarded the DSC.

10   TNA ADM 1/10573: Operation XD (Party D Antwerp) (1940).

11   *LG* (11 July 1940).

12   Thompson, John, *HMS Lively: A Brief History of an L Class Destroyer* (Accessed via www.ahoy.tk-jk.net/HMSLivelyBook).

13   *LG* (20 February 1942).
14   Quoted in Thompson, *HMS Lively*.
15   TNA ADM 1/11947: Board of Inquiry into the losses of HMS *Neptune* and HMS *Kandahar*. Accessed online at www.hmsneptune.com.
16   Brookes, Ewart, *Destroyer* (Arrow, 1973), p. 196.
17   Brookes, *Destroyer*, p. 198.
18   Kemp, Paul, *The Admiralty Regrets: British Warship Losses of the 20th Century* (Stroud, Sutton, 1999), p. 183.
19   Connell, G.G., *Mediterranean Maelstrom: HMS Jervis and the 14th Flotilla* (London, William Kimber, 1987), p. 162.
20   Connell, *HMS Jervis*, p. 163.
21   *LG* (8 September 1942).

5   Portsmouth's Submariners

1   Hood, Jean, *Submarine: An Anthology of First Hand Accounts of War Under Sea, 1939–45* (Conway Maritime, 2007), pp. 63, 70.
2   Gray, Edwyn, *Few Survived – A History of Submarine Disasters* (Barnsley, Leo Cooper, 1996), p. 74.
3   Gray, *Few Survived*, p. 75.
4   Hood, *Submarine*, p. 176.
5   Kemp, Paul, *The Admiralty Regrets: British Warship Losses of the 20th Century* (Stroud, Sutton, 1999), p. 101.
6   Quoted in Wragg, David, *Royal Navy Handbook 1939–1945* (Stroud, Sutton, 2006), p. 113.
7   Walters, Derek, *The History of the British U-class Submarine* (Barnsley, Leo Cooper, 2004), p. 206.
8   TNA ADM 1/19843: Henry Miller George Cross citation.
9   Evans, A.S., *Beneath the Waves: A History of HM Submarine Losses* (London, William Kimber, 1986), p. 220.
10   *LG* (16 August 1940).
11   Kemp, *The Admiralty Regrets*, p. 105.
12   Kemp, *The Admiralty Regrets*, p. 130.
13   *LG* (28 June 1940).
14   Submarines are always referred to as boats rather than as ships.
15   TNA ADM188/1089: Arthur Biggleston service record.
16   *Kelly's* (1939–40).
17   *Kelly's* (1946).
18   Wragg, *Royal Navy Handbook*, p. 104.
19   Wingate, John, *The Fighting Tenth: The Tenth Submarine Flotilla and the Siege of Malta* (Barnsley, Leo Cooper, 1991), p. 7.
20   Wingate, *The Fighting Tenth*, p. 32.
21   *LG* (16 January 1942).
22   *LG* (5 January 1942).
23   Evans, *Beneath the Waves*, p. 344.
24   *NL* (June 1937).
25   *NL* (December 1938).
26   Evans, *Beneath the Waves*, p. 344.
27   *LG* (3 April 1942).
28   *LG* (17 July 1942).
29   www.naval-history.net.
30   www.naval-history.net.
31   *LG* (1 January 1941).
32   Evans, *Beneath the Waves*, p. 344.
33   Kemp, *The Admiralty Regrets*, p. 245.
34   Hood, *Submarine*, p. 386.

6 Per Mar Per Terram: *The Royal Marines*

1 Neillands, Robin, *By Sea and Land: The Story of the Royal Marine Commandos* (London, Cassell Military, 2000), p. 7.
2 Thompson, Julian, *History of the Royal Marines: From Sea Soldiers to a Special Force* (London, Sidgwick and Jackson, 2000), p. 239.
3 Brooks, Richard, *The Royal Marines: History of the Royal Marines 1664–2000* (London, Constable, 2002), p. 250.
4 Ladd, James, *By Sea, By Land: The Royal Marines, 1919–1997: An Authorised History* (London, Collins, 1999), pp. 127, 187.
5 Brooks, *The Royal Marines*, p. 253.
6 Thompson, *History of the Royal Marines*, p. 251.
7 Ladd, *By Sea, By Land*, p. 100.
8 TNA ADM 159/32: Frederick Bird service record.
9 Trendell, John, *Operation Music-Maker: The Story of Royal Marines Bands* (privately published, 1978), p. 65.
10 Trendell, *Operation Music-Maker*, p. 66.
11 Trendell, *Operation Music-Maker*, p. 68.
12 Trendell, *Operation Music-Maker*, p. 68.
13 TNA ADM 159/199: William Rhodes service record.
14 Beadle, Jeffrey, *The Light Blue Lanyard: Fifty Years with 40 Commando Royal Marines* (Worcester, Square One, 1992), pp. 20, 26.
15 This argument focusing on Mountbatten and Dieppe is summarised in Villa, Brian Lorings, *Unauthorized Action: Mountbatten and the Dieppe Raid* (Toronto, Oxford University Press Canada, 1994).
16 Beadle, *The Light Blue Lanyard*, p. 77.
17 Brooks, *The Royal Marines*, p. 263.
18 Ladd, *By Sea, By Land*, p. 100.
19 Ford, Ken, *D-Day Commando: From Normandy to the Maas with 48 Royal Marine Commando* (Stroud, Sutton, 2003), pp. 137, 158.
20 Ladd, *By Sea, By Land*, p. 418.

7 Pompey's Tigers: *The Hampshire Regiment*

1 Gordon, Iain, *Bloodline: The Origins and Development of the Regular Formations of the British Army* (Barnsley, Pen and Sword, 2010), p. 82.
2 Mallinson, Allan, *The Making of the British Army* (London, Bantam Press, 2009), p. 325.
3 Fraser, David, *And We Shall Shock Them: The British Army in the Second World War* (London, Hodder and Staughton, 1983), p. 91.
4 The most prominent example of this was at Salerno during the Italian campaign.
5 Something, of course, which Portsmouth suffered in the Second World War with the loss of HMS *Royal Oak*, HMS *Hood* and HMS *Barham*.
6 French, David, *Raising Churchill's Army: The British Army and the War against Germany 1919–1945* (Oxford, University Press, 2001), p. 146.
7 Scott Daniell, David, *Regiment History of the Royal Hampshire Regiment, Volume III, 1918–1954* (Aldershot, Gale and Polden, 1955). Two other battalions fought as armour and artillery. Unless otherwise noted information about the Hampshire Regiment in action is taken from the Regimental History.
8 PMRS Ellis OHI 5332A.
9 Wragg, David, *Malta: The Last Great Siege 1940–1943* (Barnsley, Pen and Sword, 2006).
10 Scott Daniell, *Royal Hampshire Regiment 1918–1954*, pp. 91–8.
11 *LG* (11 January 1944).
12 TNA WO 373/4: Recommendation for Military Medal, Private Mark Pook.
13 PMRS Ellis OHI 5332A.

8 'Very great powers of command': Major Robert Easton DSO, MBE

1   RMAS: Admission register (1933).
2   PGS. I am indebted to the school's archivist, John Sadden, and school pupils who have researched Major Easton's life.
3   RMAS: Admission register (1933).
4   French, David, *Raising Churchill's Army: The British Army and the War against Germany 1919–1945* (Oxford, University Press, 2001), p. 50.
5   French, *Raising Churchill's Army*, p. 58.
6   *AL* (1935); *LG* (1 February 1935).
7   RMAS: Admission register (1933).
8   Fraser, David, *And We Shall Shock Them: The British Army in the Second World War* (London, Hodder and Staughton, 1983), pp. 8, 16, 19.
9   *AL* (July 1942).
10 GRO: 8c 1319 Bury, December 1939 Quarter.
11 TNA WO 166/4409: 1/6 Lancashire Fusiliers War Diary Sept 1939–Mar 1940; June 1940–Dec 1941.
12 TNA WO 167/780: 1/6 Lancashire Fusiliers War Diary Mar–May 1940.
13 *LG* (27 June 1941).
14 Fraser, *And We Shall Shock Them*, p. 100.
15 TNA WO 166/4409.
16 Fraser, *And We Shall Shock Them*, p. 84.
17 TNA WO 166/166/6929: 109 Regiment Royal Armoured Corps War Diary, Jan–Dec 1942.
18 *AL* (January 1944).
19 TNA WO 166/11102: 109 Regiment Royal Armoured Corps War Diary Jan–Dec 1943.
20 TNA WO 169/9385: 142 Regiment Royal Armoured Corps War Diary July–Dec 1943.
21 Ellis, John, *Cassino: The Hollow Victory – The Battle for Rome January–June 1944* (London, Andre Deutsch Ltd, 1994), p. 268.
22 Ellis, *Cassino*, p. 394.
23 Ellis, *Cassino*, p. 401.
24 TNA WO 373/7: Recommendation for Distinguished Service Order.
25 *LG* (24 August 1944).
26 Nicholson, Col W.N., *The History of the Suffolk Regiment 1928–46* (Naval and Military Press, 2002), p. 284.
27 *Portmuthian* (December 1944).

9 Overlord: D-Day and the Battle of Normandy

1   *Kelly's* (1938–39).
2   TNA WO 171/1305: 1st Battalion Hampshire Regiment War Diary June 1944.
3   PMRS OHI Harry Cripps OHI 5251A.
4   'DD' refers to Duplex-Drive, the tank's drive mechanism that allowed it to move in water and on land.
5   Scott Daniell, David, *Regiment History of The Royal Hampshire Regiment, Volume III, 1918–1954* (Aldershot, Gale and Polden, 1955), p. 218.
6   PMRS Cripps OHI 5251A.
7   GRO: Gosport 2b 740, June Quarter.
8   TNA WO 373/48: Leslie Webb Military Medal citation.
9   Beevor, Anthony, *D-Day: The Battle for Normandy* (London, Viking, 2009).
10 RAF Bomb Disposal Association, http://www.rafbdhistory.co.uk/new_page_3.htm.
11 Communication with Chris Cornell, Sergeant Cornell's great-nephew.
12 TNA WO 171/1239: 7th Battalion Parachute Regiment War Diary 1944. Unless otherwise noted details of Cornell's service in Normandy are taken from this War Diary.
13 Projectile Infantry Anti-Tank.
14 Maddox, Barbara, *The Tale of Two Bridges: Based on the Diary of Colonel R.G. Pine-Coffin DSO MC* (Privately Published, 2003).

15   TNA WO 373/50: Sidney Cornell Distinguished Conduct Medal citation.
16   TNA WO 171/5134: 7th Battalion Parachute Regiment War Diary 1945.
17   For a summary of these arguments, see D'este, Carlo, *Decision in Normandy: The Unwritten Story of Montgomery and the Allied Campaign* (New York, Dutton, 1983), and for the counter-arguments, see Neillands, Robin, *The Battle of Normandy 1944* (London, Orion, 2003). Montgomery was promoted to field marshal in September 1944.
18   Daglish, *Operation Epsom: Over the Battlefield* (Barnsley, Pen and Sword, 2005).
19   I am grateful to Ian Daglish for this information.
20   Delaforce, Patrick, *The Fighting Wessex Wyverns: From Normandy to Bremerhaven with the 43rd Wessex Division* (Sutton, 2003), p. 45.
21   Delaforce, *Wessex Wyverns*, pp. 74–80.
22   Daglish, *Operation Goodwood*.
23   Neillands, *The Battle for Normandy*, and D'Este, *Decision in Normandy*.
24   Daglish, *Operation Bluecoat: Over the Battlefield* (Barnsley, Pen and Sword, 2009).
25   Delaforce, *Wessex Wyverns*, p. 136.
26   French, David, *Raising Churchill's Army: The British Army and the War against Germany 1919–1945* (Oxford, University Press, 2001), p. 147.

10   Prisoners of War

1   MacArthur, Brian, *Surviving the Sword: Prisoners of the Japanese* (London, Time Warner, 2005), p. 2.
2   Gilbert, Adrian, *POW: Allied Prisoners in Europe, 1939–45* (London, John Murray, 2006), p. xi.
3   TNA WO 331/18: HQ Norway War Crimes Branch, Operation Freshman: killing of survivors at Slettebø.
4   TNA WO 311/386: Army Legal Services: Killing of survivors from Operation Freshman.
5   TNA WO 311/383: Army Legal Services: Killing of survivors from Operation Freshman.
6   TNA WO 311/387: Army Legal Services: Killing of survivors from Operation Freshman.
7   Germany and German Occupied Territories, Imperial Prisoners of War; Alphabetical Lists (HMSO, 1945), accessed online at www.findmypast.co.uk; Gilbert, *POW*, p. 83.
8   Gilbert, *POW*, p. 84.
9   Nichol, John and Rennell, Tony, *The Last Escape: The Untold Story of Allied Prisoners of War in Germany 1944–1945* (London, Viking, 2002), p. 152.
10   Correspondence with the curator of the D-Day Museum.
11   PMRS 1986/213/1-2. Pompey did indeed win 16-1 against Clapham Orient in 1942. Neasom, Mike, Cooper, Mick and Robinson, Doug, *Pompey: The History of Portsmouth Football Club* (Horndean, Milestone Publications, 1984).
12   PMRS 1986/213/1-2.
13   MacArthur, *Surviving the Sword*, p. 2.
14   Smith, Colin, *Singapore Burning: Heroism and Surrender in World War II* (London, Penguin, 2006), p. 550.
15   Information on POWs held by the Japanese is taken from the excellent Children of Far East Prisoners of War website at www.cofepow.org.uk. The COFEPOW database is based on documents in the National Archives series WO 344.
16   MacArthur, *Surviving the Sword*, p. 325.
17   MacArthur, *Surviving the Sword*, pp. 56, 111.
18   His exact date of death is unknown.
19   MacArthur, *Surviving the Sword*, p. 344.

11   Forgotten Army: War in the Far East

1   Smith, Colin, *Singapore Burning: Heroism and Surrender in World War II* (London, Penguin, 2006), p. 11.
2   Nesbit, Roy Conyers, *The Battle for Burma* (Barnsley, Pen and Sword, 2009), p. 24.
3   Nesbit, *The Battle for Burma*, p. 25.
4   Chinnery, Phillip, *Wingate's Lost Brigade: The First Chindit Operations 1943* (Barnsley, Pen and Sword, 2010), p. 15.

5   Chinnery, *Wingate's Lost Brigade*, p. 27.
6   Chinnery, *Wingate's Lost Brigade*, p. 61.
7   The National Archives (TNA) WO 361/442: Enquiries into Missing Personnel, 1939–45 War, 13th Battalion, King's Regiment.
8   Chinnery, *Wingate's Lost Brigade*, p. 26.
9   TNA WO 361/442.
10 Chinnery, *Wingate's Lost Brigade*, p. 162.
11 TNA WO 345/50: Japanese Index Cards of Allied Prisoners of War and Internees, Second World War.
12 All British soldiers are given a unique regimental number when they enlist, which remains with them throughout their service. These numbers are allocated in blocks, and hence even if a soldier transferred from one regiment to another their original unit can be traced.
13 TNA WO 203/2695: V Force organisation: correspondence; WO 172/4585: V Force HQ War Diary 1944.
14 TNA WO 373/42: Maurice Budd Military Cross citation.
15 LG (17 January 1946).

12 'Bucky': Wing Commander John Buchanan DSO, DFC

1   PGS. I am grateful to John Sadden, the archivist of Portsmouth Grammar School, and pupils who have researched Buchanan for this information.
2   *Flight* (12 December 1935), p. 627, and *Flight* (9 January 1936), p. 40.
3   www.unithistories.com.
4   TNA AIR 27/810: 101 Squadron Operations Record Book Mar 1928–Dec 1941.
5   LG (30 July 1940).
6   LG (1 February 1944).
7   TNA AIR 27/192: 14 Sqn Operations Record Book Sept 1939–Dec 1940; TNA AIR 27/193: 14 Sqn Operations Record Book with appendices Jan–Dec 1941.
8   LG (24 September 1941).
9   14 Squadron Association newsletter No 8, accessed via the association's website at www.14sqn-association.org.uk.
10 TNA AIR 27/193.
11 LG (7 April 1942).
12 TNA AIR 27/1577: 272 Squadron Operations Record Book Nov 1940–Dec 1942.
13 Wragg, David, *Malta: The Last Great Siege 1940–1943* (Barnsley, Pen and Sword, 2006), pp. 197, 215.
14 Wragg, *Malta*, p. 214.
15 TNA AIR 27/1579: 272 Squadron Operations Record Book 1942.
16 LG (29 December 1942).
17 TNA AIR 27/1578.
18 TNA AIR 27/1578: 227 Squadron Operations Record Book Jan 1943–Apr 1945.
19 TNA AIR 27/1409: 227 Squadron Operations Record Book Aug 1942–Dec 1943.
20 TNA AIR 27/1409.
21 PGS. Letter from RAF Historical Branch to Portsmouth Grammar School. I am grateful to the school's archivist John Sadden for this information.
22 PGS. Undated clipping from the *Portsmouth Evening News* published after Buchanan's death.
23 www.torontoaircrew.com.

13 Portsmouth's Bomber Boys

1   Flight Lieutenant John Coghlan, who was not actually flying a fighter when he was killed.
2   Terraine, John, *The Right of the Line* (Hertfordshire, Wordsworth, 1998).
3   All details of bomber losses are taken from www.lostbombers.com, which in turn is based on Middlebrook, Martin and Everitt, Chris, *The Bomber Command War Diaries: An Operational Reference Book 1939–1945* (Leicester, Midland Publishing, 2006).

4   *LG* (2 September 1941).
5   Probert, Henry, *Bomber Harris: His Life and Times* (Barnsley, Greenhill, 2006).
6   Portsmouth Electricity Service plaque in Portsmouth cathedral. I am grateful to www.
     memorialsinportsmouth.com for this information.
7   TNA AIR 50/185: Sergeant Francis Compton Combat Report 24/25 June 1943.
8   TNA AIR 27/144: 10 Squadron Operations Record Book January–December 1943.
9   Wragg, David, *Royal Air Force Handbook 1939–1945* (Stroud, Sutton, 2007), p. 125.
10   Wilson, Kevin, *Bomber Boys: The Ruhr, the Dambusters and Bloody Berlin* (London, Cassell Military,
     2006), pp. 125–45.
11   Bomber Command War Diary Apr 1943, via www.raf.mod.uk/bombercommand.
12   Bomber Command War Dairy May 1943, via www.raf.mod.uk/bombercommand.
13   TNA AIR 27/144.
14   TNA AIR 27/144; TNA AIR 50/180: Sergeant Francis Compton Combat Report 15 May 1943.
15   *LG* (4 June 1943).
16   TNA AIR 27/380: 35 Squadron Operations Record Book January–December 1943.
17   Wilson, *Bomber Boys*, pp. 282–316; and Terraine, *The Right of the Line*, p. 541.
18   Wilson, *Bomber Boys*, pp. 317–39.
19   *LG* (11 February 1944).
20   Terraine, *The Right of the Line*, pp. 623–4.
21   TNA AIR 27/101: 7 Squadron Operations Record Book January–December 1944.
22   Wragg, *RAF Handbook*, p. 119.

14   'Nine Gun': Flight Lieutenant John Coghlan DFC

1   PGS. I am indebted to John Sadden, the school's archivist, for information about Coghlan's time at
     the school and subsequent career.
2   *Kelly's* (1938–39).
3   Commonwealth War Graves Commission Online Debt of Honour Register, www.cwgc.org.
4   TNA AIR 4/17: Pilot's Flying Log Book J.H. Coghlan.
5   *AFL* (March 1937).
6   *AFL* (June 1937).
7   *AFL* (May 1938).
8   *AFL* (November 1938).
9   TNA AIR 4/17.
10   http://www.northwealdairfieldhistory.org/content/battle-barking-creek.
11   TNA AIR 27/528: 56 Squadron Operations Record Book (Jan–Dec 1940).
12   TNA AIR 4/17.
13   Eric Clayton, What if the Heavens Fall: Reminiscences of 56(F) Squadron in the Battle of Britain
     (Privately Published, 1993).
14   TNA AIR 50/22/654: Aerial Combat Report J.H. Coghlan.
15   TNA AIR 27/528.
16   TNA AIR 27/528; TNA AIR 50/22/654.
17   TNA AIR 50/22/654.
18   TNA AIR 50/22/654.
19   TNA AIR 50/22/655: Aerial Combat Report J.H. Coghlan.
20   TNA AIR 50/22/655.
21   TNA AIR 50/22/655.
22   TNA AIR 50/22/656: Aerial Combat Report J.H. Coghlan.
23   TNA AIR 50/22/657: Aerial Combat Report J.H. Coghlan.
24   *LG* (30 July 1940).
25   TNA AIR 4/17.
26   TNA AIR 27/534: 56 Squadron Operations Record Book Appendices (Jan–Dec 1940).
27   TNA AIR 27/528.

28   TNA AIR 4/17.
29   Clayton, *What if the Heavens Fall*.
30   *LG* (17 February 1942).

15   *Brothers in Arms: The Venables Brothers*

1   Information received from Stephen Harding-Morris.
2   TNA AIR 27/662: 78 Squadron Operations Record Book 1945.
3   Wragg, David, *Royal Air Force Handbook 1939–1945* (Stroud, Sutton, 2007), p. 126.
4   Cummings, Colin, *The Price of Peace: A Catalogue of RAF Losses Between VE Day and the End of 1945* (Halifax, Nimbus Publishing, 2004), p. 455.
5   Cummings, *The Price of Peace*, pp. 455–6.
6   GRO: Portsmouth 2b 715, December Quarter 1945.
7   Information received from Stephen Harding-Morris.

16   *The NAAFI*

1   Cole, Howard N., *NAAFI in Uniform* (NCS/EFI Old Comrades Association, 1982), p. 132.
2   Miller, Harry, *Service to the Services: The Story of the NAAFI* (Newman Neame, 1971), p. 57.
3   Cole, *NAAFI in Uniform*, p. 148.
4   Woodward, *One Hundred Days: The Memoirs of the Falklands Battle Group Commander* (London, HarperCollins, 2003), pp. 371, 375, 378.
5   Cole, *NAAFI in Uniform*, p. 132.
6   Miller, *Service to the Services*, p. 57.
7   Information about ships is taken from www.navalhistory.net; and College, J.J. and Wardlow, Ben, *Ships of the Royal Navy: A Complete Record of All Fighting Ships from the 15th Century to the Present* (London, Chatham Publishing, 2006).
8   Cole, *NAAFI in Uniform*, p. 132.
9   Cole, *NAAFI in Uniform*, p. 141.
10   All information on ship losses is taken from Kemp, Paul, *The Admiralty Regrets: British Warship Losses of the 20th Century* (Stroud, Sutton, 1999).
11   For more information see Chapter 4.
12   Miller, *Service to the Services*, p. 46.
13   Cole, *NAAFI in Uniform*, p. 151.

17   *Women at War*

1   Harris, Carole, *Women at War 1939–1945: Britain's Women and the War Effort* (Stroud, Sutton, 2000), p. 7.
2   Wragg, David, *Royal Air Force Handbook 1939–1945* (Stroud: Sutton, 2007), p. 7.
3   PMRS Kay Childs OHI 2342A.
4   PMRS Hessie Hare OHI 2301A.
5   Patterson, Sandra E., 'The Auxiliary Territorial Service in the Second World War' (Imperial War Museum Information Sheet, No 42, 2003).
6   Stedman, John, 'Portsmouth Reborn: Destruction and Reconstruction 1941–1974' (Portsmouth Papers, 66, p. 4).
7   PMRS Jackson OHI 5323A.
8   Wragg, *Royal Navy Handbook 1939–1945*, p. 134; Escott, Beryl E., *Women in Air Force Blue: The Story of Women in the Royal Air Force from 1918 to the Present Day* (Sparkford, Patrick Stephens, 1989), p. 94.
9   Escott, *Women in Air Force Blue*, p. 100.
10   Escott, *Women in Air Force Blue*, pp. 170–2.
11   PMRS Hare OHI 2301A.
12   PMRS Childs OHI 2342A.
13   Wragg, *RAF Handbook*, pp. 135–6.
14   PMRS Nancy Jackson OHI 5323A.

18 *The Merchant Navy*

1   Edwards, Bernard, *The Quiet Heroes: British Merchant Seamen at War* (Leo Cooper, 2002), p. 1.

2   Lewis, William J., *Under the Red Duster: The Merchant Navy in World War II* (Ramsbury, Airlife Publishing, 2003), pp. 2–3.

3   Lewis, *Under the Red Duster*, p. 12.

4   Edwards, *The Quiet Heroes*, p. 172.

5   Wragg, David, *Royal Air Force Handbook 1939–1945* (Stroud, Sutton, 2007), p. 7.

6   Details of this and all other merchant shipping losses are taken from the website www.uboat.net.

7   The author can recall fishing over the wreck of the *Irishman* before it was blown up.

8   TNA BT 389/24: SS *Portsdown* Index Card.

9   PMRS Lupton Oral History Interview (OHI) 5421A.

10   Phillips, Kenneth S., *Shipwreck! Broken on the Wight* (Island Books, 1995), p. 60.

11   TNA WO 361/152: War Office Casualties at Sea: SS *Portsdown*.

12   PMRS Lupton OHI 5421A.

13   For more information on the war against the U-boats see Terraine, John, *Business in Great Waters* (Barnsley, Pen and Sword, 2009), p. 864.

Bibliography

Primary Sources

Barking and Dagenham Library (BDL).

General Register Office (GRO): birth, marriage and death records.

The National Archives: Admiralty (ADM) 1, 159, 178, 188, 196; Air Ministry (AIR) 4, 27, 50; Board of Trade (BT) 389; Home Office (HO) 186, 198; Prime Minister (PREM) 3; War Office (WO) 166, 167, 169, 171, 172, 203, 311, 331, 345, 361, 373.

Portsmouth Central Library (PCL): electoral registers.

Portsmouth Grammar School (PGS).

Portsmouth Museum and Records Service (PMRS): oral history interviews, 1986/213/1-2.

Royal Military Academy Sandhurst (RMAS): admission registers.

Books

Beadle, Jeffrey, *The Light Blue Lanyard: Fifty Years with 40 Commando Royal Marines* (Worcester, Square One, 1992).

Beevor, Anthony, *D-Day: The Battle for Normandy* (London, Viking, 2009).

Bradford, Ernle, *The Mighty Hood* (The Book Service, 1974).

Brookes, Ewart, *Destroyer* (Arrow, 1973).

Brooks, Richard, *The Royal Marines: History of the Royal Marines 1664–2000* (London, Constable, 2002).

Cashford, Noel, *Bang! Stories of Bangs from 1917 to the Present Day* (Sheffield, ALD Print, 2008).

Chinnery, Phillip, *Wingate's Lost Brigade: The First Chindit Operations 1943* (Barnsley, Pen and Sword, 2010).

Clayton, Eric, *What if the Heavens Fall: Reminiscences of 56(F) Squadron in the Battle of Britain* (Privately Published, 1993).

Cole, Howard N., *NAAFI in Uniform* (NCS/EFI Old Comrades Association, 1982).

College, J.J. and Wardlow, Ben, *Ships of the Royal Navy: A Complete Record of All Fighting Ships from the 15th Century to the Present* (London, Chatham Publishing, 2006).

Connell, G.G., *Mediterranean Maelstrom: HMS Jervis and the 14th Flotilla* (London William Kimber, 1987).

Cummings, Colin, *The Price of Peace: A Catalogue of RAF Losses Between VE Day and the End of 1945* (Halifax, Nimbus Publishing, 2004).

Cunningham, Admiral Sir A.N., *A Sailor's Odyssey* (London, Hutchinson, 1952).

Daglish, I., *Operation Epsom: Over the Battlefield* (Barnsley, Pen and Sword, 2005).

———, *Operation Goodwood: Over the Battlefield* (Barnsley, Pen and Sword, 2005).

———, *Operation Bluecoat: Over the Battlefield* (Barnsley, Pen and Sword, 2009).

D'este, Carlo, *Decision in Normandy: The Unwritten Story of Montgomery and the Allied Campaign* (New York, Dutton, 1983).

Delaforce, Patrick, *The Fighting Wessex Wyverns: From Normandy to Bremerhaven with the 43rd Wessex Division* (Stroud, Sutton, 2003).

Edwards, Bernard, *The Quiet Heroes: British Merchant Seamen at War* (Leo Cooper, 2002).

Ellis, John, *Cassino: The Hollow Victory – The Battle for Rome, January–June 1944* (London, Andre Deutsch Ltd, 1994).

Escott, Beryl E., *Women in Air Force Blue: The Story of Women in the Royal Air Force from 1918 to the Present Day* (Sparkford, Patrick Stephens, 1989).

Evans, A.S., *Beneath the Waves – A History of HM Submarine Losses* (London, William Kimber, 1986).

Ford, Ken, *D-Day Commando: From Normandy to the Maas with 48 Royal Marine Commando* (Stroud, Sutton, 2003).

Fraser, David, *And We Shall Shock Them: The British Army in the Second World War* (London, Hodder and Staughton, 1983).

French, David, *Raising Churchill's Army: The British Army and the War against Germany 1919–1945* (Oxford University Press, 2001).

Gilbert, Adrian, *POW: Allied prisoners in Europe, 1939–45* (London, John Murray, 2006).

Gordon, Iain, *Bloodline: The Origins and Development of the Regular Formations of the British Army* (Barnsley, Pen and Sword, 2010).

Gray, Edwyn, *Few Survived – A History of Submarine Disasters* (Barnsley, Leo Cooper, 1996).

Harris, Carole, *Women at War 1939–1945: Britain's Women and the War Effort* (Stroud, Sutton, 2000).

Hood, Jean, *Submarine: An Anthology of First Hand Accounts of War Under Sea, 1939–45* (Conway Maritime, 2007).

Hoyt, Edwin P., *The Life and Death of HMS Hood* (Littlehampton Book Services, 1977).

Jones, Geoffrey, *Battleship Barham* (William Kimber, 1979).

Kemp, Paul, *The Admiralty Regrets: British Warship Losses of the 20th Century* (Stroud, Sutton, 1999).

Ladd, James, *By Sea, By Land: The Royal Marines, 1919–1997: An Authorised History* (London, Collins, 1999).

Lewis, William J., *Under the Red Duster: The Merchant Navy in World War II* (Ramsbury, Airlife Publishing, 2003).

MacArthur, Brian, *Surviving the Sword: Prisoners of the Japanese* (London, Time Warner, 2005).

Maddox, Barbara, *The Tale of Two Bridges: Based on the Diary of Colonel R.G. Pine-Coffin DSO MC* (Privately Published, 2003).

Mallinson, Allan, *The Making of the British Army* (London, Bantam Press, 2009).

McKee, Alexander, *Black Saturday: The Tragedy of the Royal Oak* (Souvenir Press, 1959).

Millar, John, *A Portrait of a Family* (Privately Published).

Miller, Harry, *Service to the Services: The Story of the NAAFI* (Newman Neame, 1971).

Neasom, Mike, Cooper, Mick and Robinson, Doug, *Pompey: The History of Portsmouth Football Club* (Horndean, Milestone Publications, 1984).

Neillands, Robin, *By Sea and Land: The Story of the Royal Marine Commandos* (London, Cassell Military, 2000).

———, *The Battle of Normandy 1944* (London, Orion, 2003).

Nesbit, Roy Conyers, *The Battle for Burma* (Barnsley, Pen and Sword, 2009).

Nichol, John and Rennell, Tony, *The Last Escape: The Untold Story of Allied Prisoners of War in Germany, 1944–1945* (London, Viking, 2002).

Nicholson, Col W.N., *The History of the Suffolk Regiment 1928–1946* (Naval and Military Press, 2002).

Norman, Andrew, *HMS Hood: Pride of the Royal Navy* (Gloucestershire, Spellmount, 2002).

Owen, James, *Danger UXB: The Heroic Story of the WWII Bomb Disposal Teams* (London, Little, Brown, 2010).

Phillips, Kenneth S., *Shipwreck! Broken on the Wight* (Island Books, 1995).

Phillipson, David, *Band of Brothers: Boy Seamen in the Royal Navy, 1800–1956* (Stroud, Sutton, 1996).

Probert, Henry, *Bomber Harris: His Life and Times* (Barnsley, Greenhill, 2006).

Scott Daniell, David, *Regiment History of the Royal Hampshire Regiment, Volume III, 1918–1954* (Aldershot, Gale and Polden, 1955).

Smith, Colin, *Singapore Burning: Heroism and Surrender in World War II* (London, Penguin, 2006).

Snyder, Gerald S., *The Royal Oak Disaster* (William Kimber, 1976).

Sugden, John, *Nelson: A Dream of Glory* (London, Jonathan Cape, 2004).

Terraine, John, *The Right of the Line* (Hertfordshire, Wordsworth, 1998).

———, *Business in Great Waters* (Barnsley, Pen and Sword, 2009).

Thompson, Julian, *History of the Royal Marines: From Sea Soldiers to a Special Force* (London, Sidgwick and Jackson, 2000).

Trendell, John, *Operation Music-Maker: The Story of Royal Marines Bands* (Privately Published, 1978).

Turner, David, *Last Dawn: The Royal Oak Tragedy at Scapa Flow* (Glendaruel, Argyll Publishing, 2009).

Turner, John Frayn, *Awards of the George Cross 1940–2005* (Barnsley, Pen and Sword, 2010).

Villa, Brian Lorings, *Unauthorized Action: Mountbatten and the Dieppe Raid* (Toronto, Oxford University Press Canada, 1994).

Walters, Derek, *The History of the British U-class Submarine* (Barnsley, Leo Cooper, 2004).

Whitmarsh, Andrew, *Portsmouth at War* (Stroud, Tempus, 2007).

Wilson, Kevin, *Bomber Boys: The Ruhr, the Dambusters and Bloody Berlin* (London, Cassell Military, 2006).

Wingate, John, *The Fighting Tenth: The Tenth Submarine Flotilla and the Siege of Malta* (Barnsley, Leo Cooper, 1991).

Woodward, *One Hundred Days: The Memoirs of the Falklands Battle Group Commander* (London, HarperCollins, 2003).

Wragg, David, *Royal Navy Handbook 1939–1945* (Stroud, Sutton, 2006).

———, *Malta: The Last Great Siege 1940–1943* (Barnsley, Pen and Sword, 2006).

———, *Royal Air Force Handbook 1939–1945* (Stroud, Sutton, 2007), p.125.

Journals and Magazines Articles

Lockwood, Martyn, 'The End of the Phoney War' (Essex Police Museum History Notebook, No 26).

Patterson, Sandra E., 'The Auxiliary Territorial Service in the Second World War' (Imperial War Museum Information Sheet, No 42, 2003).

Stedman, John, 'Portsmouth Reborn: Destruction and Reconstruction 1941–1974' (Portsmouth Papers, No 66, 1994).

Stevenson, Jason, 'The Barham Conspiracy' (*World War II Magazine*, December 2004).

Newspapers and Periodicals

Air Force List
Army List
Barking and Dagenham Recorder
Flight
Kelly's Portsmouth Directories
London Gazette
Navy List
The Portmuthian
Portsmouth Evening News
The Times

Websites

www.14sqn-association.org.uk – 14 Squadron Association
www.ahoy.tk-jk.net/HMSLivelyBook – Mac's Web Log: HMS *Lively*

www.cofepow.org.uk – Children of Far East Prisoners of War
www.combinedops.com – Combined Operations
www.cwgc.org – Commonwealth War Graves Commission
www.findmypast.co.uk – Find my Past
www.flickr.com/people/iainmclauchlan – Flickr user Iain McLauchlan
www.flickr.com/people/stephenpoole – Flickr user Stavioni
www.freebmd.org.uk – Free birth, marriage and death indexes
www.hansard.millbanksystems.com – Hansard
www.historicalrfa.org – RFA Historical Society
www.hmsbarham.com – HMS *Barham* Association
www.hmshood.com – HMS *Hood* Association
www.hmsroyaloak.co.uk – HMS *Royal Oak*
www.hongkongwardiary.com/hkwdhome.html – Hong Kong War Diary
www.hut-six.co.uk/cgi-bin/search39-47.php – Geoff's Second World War search engine
www.london-gazette.co.uk – *London Gazette*
www.lostbombers.co.uk – database of lost bombers
www.northwealdairfieldhistory.org – North Weald Airfield history
www.memorialsinportsmouth.com – Memorials in Portsmouth
www.navalhistory.net – naval history
www.ordersofbattle.com – orders of battle
www.paradata.org.uk – para database
www.pegasusarchive.com – Pegasus archive
www.raf.mod.uk/bombercommand – RAF Bomber Command
www.rafbdhistory.co.uk – RAF Bomb Disposal Association
www.rafweb.org – RAF web
www.stephen-stratford.co.uk – Stephen Stratford's Study Room
www.torontoaircrew.com – Toronto aircrew
www.uboat.net – U-boat informaton
www.unithistories.com – unit histories

Index

Aldridge, Henry (Copnor) 111
Aldridge, Henry (Landport) 83
Ambler, Edward 53
Anslow, Stanley 75
Attfield, Ernest 76
Ayling, Frank 110
Ayling, Leslie 111

Bacon, Ernest 83
Bailey, Ernest 77
Baird, Robert 125
Banks, John 43
Bannier, Stanley 78
Batterham, Henry 75
Bayliss, Marjorie 114
Beabey, Lorenzo 56
Bealing, Frederick 23–4, 26
Benford, Lawrence 83
Bennett, Kathleen 114
Benney, Charles 26
Bevan, Sidney 45
Biggleston, Arthur 45–6
Bird, Frederick 50–1
Bishop, Edward 29
Bishop, Montague 68
Blake, David 80
Bonney, Robert 79
Botting, Joyce 117
Brading, Reginald 124
Bradley, Arthur 53
Bravington, Harold 83
Broad, Benjamin 75
Buchanan, John 87–91
Buck, Arthur 30

Buck, Herbert 30
Buckner, Alfred 57
Budd, Maurice 85
Burgess, Seth 122
Burness, Michael 69
Burnett, Edwin 122
Burrows, Keith 96
Butler, George 52

Carrington, Dennis 95
Carter, Peggy 114
Chapman, George 57
Chapman, Joyce 114
Chard, Ronald 51
Charles, Frederick 53
Chinneck Bernard 57
Clarke, Herbert 99
Cockburn, Alexander 44
Cockles, Frank 83
Coghlan, John 100–5
Cole, Victor 83
Coles, Frederick 111
Collison, Frank 45–6
Compton, Francis 93–5, 96
Cooper, Gladys 114
Cooper, Norman 95–6
Cornell, Sidney 70–2
Cottrell, Edward 122
Cottrell, Walter 80
Copping, Ronald 124
Crocker, William 120

Daniels, Leslie 73
Daysh, Alan 110

Denmead, Arthur 80
Denny, Lesley 52
Derrick, Frederick 53
Dixon–Wright, Frank 93
Donachie, Eric 78
Drew, Gordon 83
Duke, Colin 120
Dunn, Jack 69
Dunstane, William 45

Easton, Robert 61–6
Edney, Arthur 45
Edwards, Cecil 78
Ellingworth, Reginald 15–22, 33–4, 44
Erridge, Albert 51
Evans, George 96
Eyres, Charles 34

Fairbrace, Percy 43
Farey, Alfred 122
Field, Ethel 114
Fitzgerald, Edward 73
Ford, Albert 45
Ford, Dennis 47
Ford, Edward 99
Foster, Derek 80
Frampton, Bertram 60
Franckeiss, Edward 26
French, Walter 83
Freshwater, Stanley 123
Fuller, Ernest 124

Garnham, George 35
Gibson, William 124
Gillard, George 56
Gleave, Frederick 52
Goff, Jack 35
Goldring, William 85
Gough, Charles 68
Green, Doug 31
Green, Ray 31

Hammond, James 80
Hansford, Walter 75
Harfield, Rita 117
Hargrave, Alan 96–8
Harriman, Reginald 50
Harris, Dorothy 114
Harrison, William 120
Hayes, John 58
Hayter, Percy 75
Hendry, George 72–3
Henley, Roy 69
Henwood, James 111
Hill, Kenneth 77
Hodge, Walter 79
Hogg, Louis 60

Horner, Charles 93
Hubbard, Clarence 47
Hudson, Frank 80
Huggins, Gordon 110
Hussey, William 34, 36–41, 111
Hyde, Arthur 60

Jago, Ernest 111
Jarman, William 57
Jay, Arthur 35
Jelley, Lesley 34
Jenkins, Williams 59
Johns, Robert 69
Johnson, Arthur 79
Joyce, Donald 51
Joyce, Lesley 35
Jones, Albert 50
Justice, Victor 59

Karmy, John 78
Keast, Lesley 92
Kehoe, Edward 79
Kennard, Harold 80–1
Kent, Ronald 69
Kewell, John 44
Kilford, George 69
Knight, Harold 83

Lamb, Jack 35
Lambard, William 50
Lambert, Charles 46–7
Lanyon, Kenneth 77
Leppard, Audrey 115
Lewis, Harry 85
Lewis, Leslie 96
Lewis, Winnifred 115
Loader, Edgar 68
Lofting, Albert 120
Longland, Norman 52
Lowlett, Norman 96
Lovell, Henry 85
Lucie, Enid 115
Luff, Roy 69
Lyons, David 76

Maker, John 50
Marchant, Frederick 56
Marshall, John 44
Martin, James 60
Matheson, Harold 109
Matthews, Lionel 111
May, Herbert 56
McCarthy, Patrick 96–8
McCauley, Thomas 47
McKormick, Joseph 93
Meehan, Kenneth 74, 96
Milbourne, Raymond 52

Miller, George 50
Miller, Henry 33–4, 44
Mills, Charles 60
Modin, Clive 74
Monk, John 122
Moore, John 80
Morey, John 80
Morgan, Percy 45
Morrell, Albert 69
Morris, Leonard 125
Morrison, Campbell 123
Moxham, Henry 79

Nimetty, Frederick 58
Nobes, John 60
Noyce, James 111
Newman, Thomas 79

Ogden, Gordon 34
Ogle, George 80–1
O'Bree, Harry 96
O'Leary, Ronald 73
Oughton, Harry 59

Paice, Harold 24, 26
Paumier, John 50
Pearce, John 77
Pharoah, Sydney 57
Phillips, William 73
Pease, Elliot 60
Phillips, Vincent 59
Pinniger, William 59
Pook, Mark 58
Preece, Sidney 57
Prince, Frederick 56
Purrington, Arthur 95

Randell, James 57
Rawlins, Bertram 122
Read, Alan 80
Rex, Edward 80
Rhodes, William 51–2
Rich, Sidney 80
Richards, Alfred 76
Robinson, Alfred 92
Roe, Frank 51
Rogers, Percival 123
Rowthorn, Peter 96
Russell, Herbert 45
Ryan, Kerry 83

Sammells, Harold 92
Sampson, Violet 116–7
Sandford, Frederick 25–6
Scott, Leslie 72

Scott, Mabel 115
Searle, Edward 60
Searle, William 57
Sly, Leonard 111
Smith, Albert 60
Smith, Archibald 44–5
Smith, Edward 58
Smith, Frederick 83
Southwell, Frederick 83
Spalding, Robert 34
Spittles, Evelyn 115
Sporne, Oscar 95
Starling, William 77–8
Stokes, Geoffrey 95
Sullivan, George 84–5
Summers, Ernest 44

Taylor, Albert 47
Teasdale, Alfred 75
Tickell, Robert 123
Tindall, Alfred 53
Tolcher, George 56
Trescothic, Herbert 92
Tuckwood, William 26
Turnbull, George 69

Usmar, Edward 31
Usmar, Harry 31

Venables, Arthur 108–9
Venables, Guy 108–9
Vince, Walter 124
Vincent, Norman 95

Walker, Cecil 27, 34
Ware, Charles 53
Watson, Leslie 96
Watts, Thomas 79
Webb, Frederick 85
Webb, Leslie 67–9
Welsh, Bertie 79
West, Alfred 110
White, Harold 110
White, Robert 57
White, William 75
Whitehead, John 95
Whitehorn, Raymond 35
Williams, Cyril 95
Williams, David 68
Williams, Edward 60
Wilson, Leonard 44
Wood, Harry 45
Woodruff, Dennis 95

Yale, John 83

Other titles published by The History Press

If War Should Come
PHILIP MACDOUGALL

£16.99

Focusing on the front-line counties of Hampshire, Sussex and Kent, the author reveals a shocking story of lost opportunity and incompetence. Using original research, he looks at plans for the emergency services, food supplies, the ARP, dispersal of industry and government, and how effective these preparations were after the outbreak of war. This is a must-read book for anyone interested in British wartime history and local historians alike.

978-0-7524-5073-5

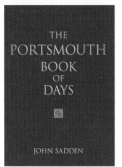

The Portsmouth Book of Days
JOHN SADDEN

£9.99

Taking you through the year day by day, this book contains a quirky, eccentric, amusing or important event or fact from different periods of history, many of which had a major impact on the religious and political history of England as a whole. Ideal for dipping into, it features hundreds of snippets of information gleaned from the vaults of Portsmouth's archives, delighting residents and visitors alike.

978-0-7524-5765-9

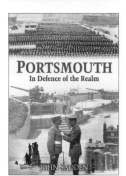

Portsmouth: In Defence of the Realm
JOHN SADDEN

£15.99

On both sides of the harbour, Pompey's fortifications, military garrison, dockyard, naval and air defence establishments, and more, are featured in this enthralling history. Not confined to the evolution of facilities and fortifications, locally developed defensive and offensive innovations and important individuals are also explored. Well illustrated, this book is essential to interested residents and visitors and to naval and military historians everywhere.

978-1-8607-7649-6

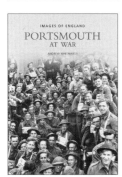

Portsmouth at War
ANDREW WHITMARSH

£12.99

This book uses nearly 200 photographs to illustrate events in Portsmouth from 1939 to 1945, also covering the post-war reconstruction of the city. Above all it is about the experiences of the city's people: air raid wardens, nurses, the Home Guard, firemen, war workers, evacuees, the Woman's Voluntary Service, those made homeless by bombing, the armed services and many others.

978-0-7524-4296-9

Visit our website and discover thousands of other History Press books.

www.thehistorypress.co.uk

The History Press